NORTH WALES IN THE MAKING

North Wales in the Making

a guide to the area's early history

Michael Senior

First edition: 1995
New edition: 2003

ISBN: 0-86381-828-5

Cover design: Sian Parri

Illustrations by Bwrdd Croeso Cymru:
Cover: Dolbadarn Castle
Back cover: Harlech castle; Castell y Bere and
Caernarfon Castle and town

First published in 1995 by
Gwasg Carreg Gwalch, 12 Iard yr Orsaf, Llanrwst, Wales LL26 0EH
01492 642031 01492 641502
books@carreg-gwalch.co.uk Internet: www.carreg-gwalch.co.uk

Contents

Author's Preface

From the window where I sit to write, looking straight ahead I see the whole of the medieval town of Conwy, its castle and town walls, quay and Victorian terraces. I can see the two famous bridges, Telford's older one largely masked from here by Stephenson's more obtrusive tube. Just out of sight to the right I am aware of the presence of the Vardre at Deganwy, the site of Conwy's predecessor fort and of many fortresses before, stretching back in a 1,500 year line to the old kingdoms of North Wales.

Above Conwy the Town Mountain rises in the centre of my view, the site of an Iron Age hillfort, the stone ring of which I can just make out, and another such fort is within sight too, to my left, on the round hilltop of Pen y Gaer above the Conwy valley. Up the slope across from Pen y Gaer rises the route of the Roman road, itself following an ancient trackway lined with Bronze Age cairns and Stone Age megaliths.

The river which runs below them, in a course smoothed by old erosions, drains the glacial cwms and ice-furrowed flanks of mountains which are among the oldest in the world.

We live, in North Wales, in an old landscape. Its intricate field patterns are derived from old social customs of inheritance, mellowed by the accident of their many hedgerow trees. Its little white farms are the legacy of an agricultural boom, but their siting probably tells us something geological, to do with the incidence of springs and wells. If little has changed about this view since this window in front of which I sit to write came to be here, virtually nothing has changed since I first saw the view myself, more than forty years ago.

Every day the estuarial river ebbs and flows. The clouds move across the mountains varying the seasons, the cycles of leaves and daffodils punctuate the year. At the same time rhythmic combinations of all these combine to turn change into continuity. Perhaps in the long view history can be seen like that, like tidal movements or the succession of winter and spring.

Certainly one of the messages of this book is durability, the way the underlying nature of the country survives intact the occurrence of often momentous events which stir its surface texture.

If North Wales has greater fascination than many places, it is partly because of the greater range of its past; but it is more essentially, perhaps, because it was always highly complex in form and foundation in any case.

What makes North Wales distinct, even to the casual observer, is the dense variety of its landscape. We shall be taking a look, in the first chapter, at the geological background to that. The ancient roots of its settlement pattern will be approached there too, and their development into recognisable forms of habitation concerns us in the second chapter. The Romans set out the main lines of communication and laid the pattern for future invasions, and their presence is recorded in the third chapter. Independent North Wales survived assaults from the sea on their departure, and its kingdoms, which concern us in the fourth chapter, lie at the origins of the power of its later rulers.

North Wales owes something of its avid independence of character, as well as many of its fortifications, to its relations with its neighbours to the east, and the complexity of this will concern us in the fifth chapter. Its elaboration into a full medieval maze of cross-relationships and intra-family feuds we shall describe, and unravel, in the sixth. In the seventh we see the final outcome, due mainly to the determined imperialism, and undoubted ability, of King Edward I.

Knowing the depth of history which lies behind the surface texture of the land gives one a new view of it even as it is now. You see behind its landscape and its built environment the age-long process which has made it the way it is.

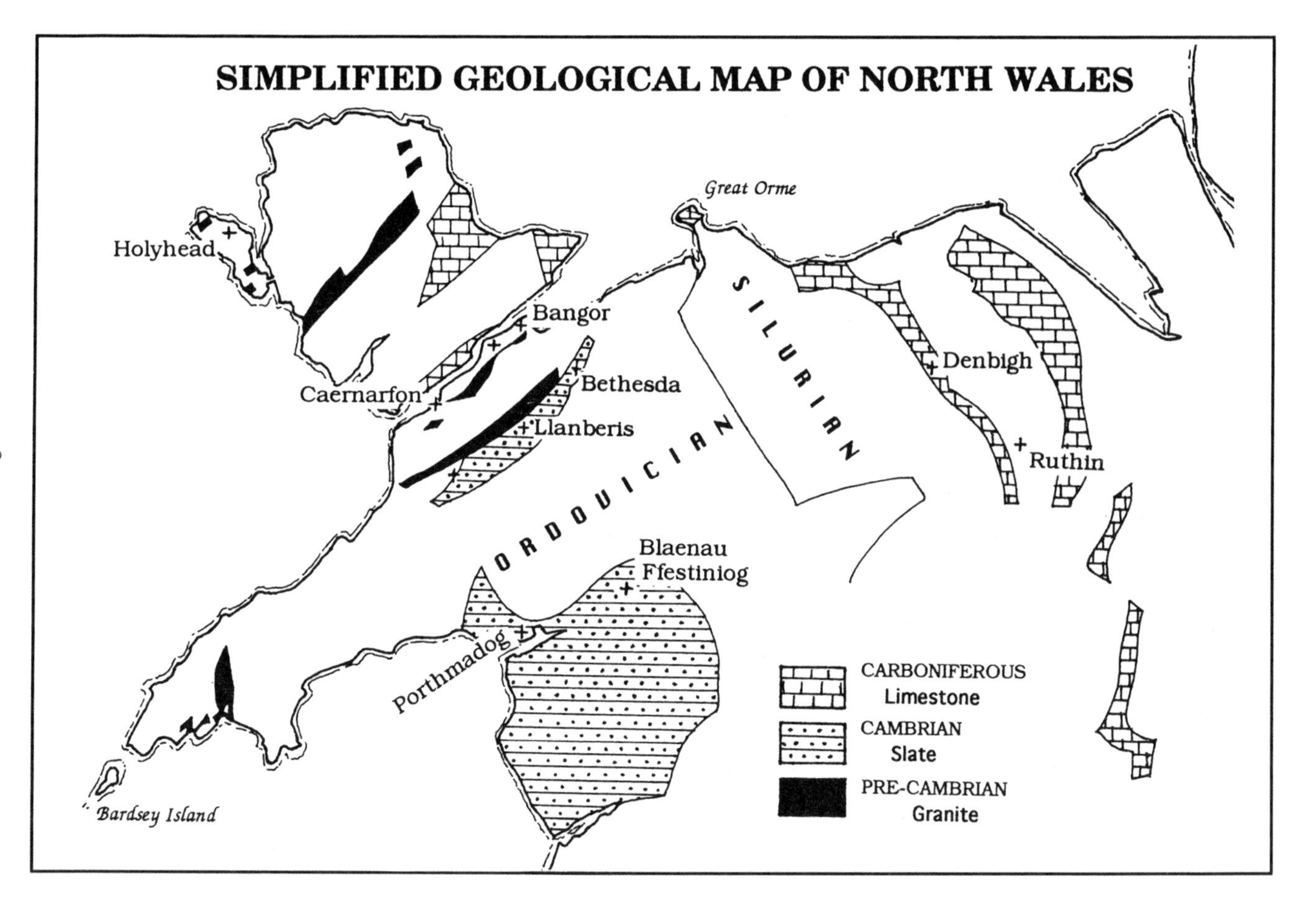
SIMPLIFIED GEOLOGICAL MAP OF NORTH WALES
Holyhead
Great Orme
Bangor
Caernarfon
Bethesda
Llanberis
SILURIAN
ORDOVICIAN
Denbigh
Ruthin
Blaenau
Ffestiniog
Porthmadog
Bardsey Island
CARBONIFEROUS
Limestone
CAMBRIAN
Slate
PRE-CAMBRIAN
Granite

First Marks on an Old Land

North Wales' richly varied present scenery is a product of its age and the variety of its rock structure. The height and sharpness of the mountains, for instance, is directly related to the hardness of the rock which composes them, itself correlated to the rock's age.

Working backwards, the most recent rocks were deposited during a period known as the Mesozoic, between 135 and 225 million years ago. These, known as New Red Sandstone, occur in our area as it meets the English border, and may be plentifully seen on the Cheshire side of that. These younger and softer rocks give rise to the gentle rolling country, providing features such as the Cheshire and Shropshire plains.

Shortly before them come the limestones, laid down in warm shallow seas by precipitation of calcium carbonite and by the deposition of the shells of millions of minute sea creatures, about 300 million years ago. A great belt of limestone outcrops runs through our area, which one can easily see by simple observation, characterised as it is by great stratified, eroded headlands and escarpments of brilliant white rock. These outcrops show at Penmon Head, in Anglesey, and of course across the bay in the fine examples of the Great and Little Ormes, the belt then running along the coast to the limestone quarrying country around Llanddulas and towards Rhuddlan, curving inland to culminate eventually in the Eliseg crags above Llangollen. Though slightly more durable than sandstone, it is the liability of limestone to erosion that has given the landform these sudden drops from escarpment to valley floor.

The moorlands, such as the Denbigh moors, are largely based on grits and shales which have been laid down as sediments, themselves eroded from older rock, such as that known as Silurian which outcrops as the basic structure of the Harlech dome and thence runs towards mid-Wales. The plateaux which these sediments form may rise to high points, but lack the resistance required to form peaks. Sediments from harder and older rocks, such as the Cambrian series, give rough craggy country, rugged rather than mountainous. The mountains themselves are formed out of the bedrock from which the sediments came.

We are now into a period known as the Palaeozoic, which is divided further into Upper (meaning younger) and Lower. The basic rocks which make the North Wales hills belong to the Lower period. Silurian rocks, as we have mentioned, feature here mainly in the Harlech dome; they emerged from the earth's core some 435 million years ago. Of most interest to us are the Ordovician rocks, composed of lava compressed between two belts of older rocks, which have given us the impressing peaks of our main mountains. These, dated at about 500 million years of age, are resistant to erosion and so remain at the highest levels and form the sharpest peaks. Yr Wyddfa and Cader Idris, for instance, display clearly the character of their Ordovician makeup.

North of the Harlech dome in the south part of the mountain ranges of North Wales lie even older rocks. These, known as Cambrian, form the great slate beds of the Llanberis, Bethesda and Ffestiniog areas. At an age of 600 million years they are the oldest of the Lower Palaeozoic rocks. Yet there is something in our geology even older. 'Pre-Cambrian' rocks are in a class of their own; at 4,500 million years they are in effect the age of the earth itself. In Britain they are found in Scotland, particularly in the Hebrides and the coast near Aberdeen. In other continents they form the beds of mineral seams, such as the iron and copper ores of North America and the gold reefs of South Africa. And they occur in a few highly characterful examples in North Wales.

Most notable among these is the group known as the 'Mona complex', which is especially evident at South Stack, the extreme jut of Anglesey into the Irish Sea. A similar outcrop appears at the end of the Lleyn peninsula. Two other of these belts of pre-Cambrian rock break surface in our area, one known as the 'Bangor ridge' running between Bangor and Caernarfon, and the other parallel to it known as the 'Padarn ridge', between Bethesda and Caernarfon Bay. Pre-Cambrian stone, as may easily be seen, is remarkable for the dense degree of its folding and for its complexity of form. The form of these rocks in fact immediately testifies to their age. They display the fact that they have survived through violent upheavals in the early history of the earth.

The actual shape of our country is due to several groups of effects. There are to begin with the effects of movements from within the earth, and we can distinguish two types of these. There have been vast upthrustings due to pressure from the earth's depths, with the rocks declining again under their own weight when the pressure is reduced. This gives rise to folding and buckling, and explains the generally undulating lie of the land. Then there is the more immediately violent effect of volcanic eruption. In North Wales the Ordovician rocks are volcanic in origin, whereas the older, and so much-folded underlays of

Cambrian and Silurian are not. Much of Snowdonia, composed of Ordovician rock, is volcanic, and hence actually composed of compressed lava, a rock form generally known as rhyolite, which characteristically fragments into boulders and breaks down further into shale.

These major activities of the earth's crust under pressure from the rumblings at its core give the underlying form of the country. The surface of it is affected yet again by two other main groups of activity, deposition and erosion.

Deposits started early, and account for the shape of much of North Wales. They included (as we saw) the laying down of the sandstone and limestone. They occurred again, in very different form, at the end of the ice ages. It was those cataclysms themselves which had the most immediately recognisable impact.

Changes in climate occur on the earth as a result of solar activity, the number of sun spots and the speed of their formation leading to lower temperature. This is not a simple progression, and change takes an oscillating, rather than a linear, form both in the long term and in shorter phases within that. There have been several ice ages in North Wales, a major one 26,000 years ago, and the greatest of all, when most of Northern Europe was for a time covered by an ice sheet over 1,400 feet thick, occurring 18,000 years ago.

Much of Britain was then under ice, and North Wales was a main ice centre. The ice started to retreat with a gradual rise in temperature starting 12,500 years ago, first leaving the lower slopes; but its decline was checked by climatic reversals, one 11,000 years ago and another lasting 700 years from 10,700 ago. With that over, the ice ages may be said to have ended in North Wales, some 10,000 years ago.

Although as mentioned one of the effects of the ice took the form of deposit, the main and most noticeable one was erosion. The ice worked on our mountains by aggravating weakened fractures, which were later further scoured by the run-off of melt water. It did not therefore create a new land form so much as exaggerate the existing underlying structure. An exception to this is the smoothing and scraping caused by debris carried underneath the glaciers, an abrasion facilitated by the ice's enormous weight.

The glaciers gnawed away at our mountains by undermining and weakening their rocks. The form which they most visibly produced is that of the cwm, known to geologists also as a corrie – the sheer-backed bowl with its hollow and lip which almost every mountain in North Wales seems to possess. Sliding downwards the glaciers which came off these mountains in many cases smoothed classical glacial valleys, such as the text-book case of Nant Ffrancon, characterised by their U shape and the way their spurs are cut off and their bumps evened out by the passing ice.

The rock faces which collapsed onto the glaciers which undermined them were then carried down-valley on the ice and eventually deposited where it melted. This effect gives us those heaps of boulders, known as moraine, which occur in even bands at the lower ends of valleys, in several stages due to the several meltings and reforming of the ice. From the moraines, in fact, we can see the various phases of the glaciers' retreat, the heavier debris deposited first, sand and gravel carried right down to the extreme extension of the ice.

There are, as well as the moraines, the scattered boulders, known as 'erratics', which rode either on or in the ice and were deposited where it could no longer sustain them. These again are of two types, which we may see for ourselves: those carried on top of the ice retained their sharp edges; whereas the ones underneath it, dragged along over the bedrock, are smoothed by the process.

Lakes again are a consequence of glaciation. They formed in the hollows cut by the upper glaciers, and in most cases are in the process still of reverting to marsh as they become infilled by debris and sediment.

The dating of the start of sedimentation, and therefore the end of glaciation, at about 10,000 years ago, was made possible by the technique of radiocarbon dating, the measuring of the decay of carbon 14, a radioactive isotope, in this case by means of analysis of peat deposits. As would be expected, the climate was then improving, and this broad trend continued, with a number of fluctuations within its overall pattern. The peat analysis shows us that in the earlier and cooler conditions the land of North Wales was largely covered in birch and pine, these being gradually suppressed by oak, alder and elm in more temperate times. By about 5,500 years ago the temperature had risen to an average maximum of 17°C., then fell again to today's average maximum (at sea level) of 15°. Changes in climate leading to increase and then loss of vegetation gave rise to the laying down of the great peat bogs.

The fact that there are peat beds at over 2,000 feet on the Carneddau testifies to one of these fluctuations, from warmer to cooler times. Nothing would grow there today, yet the pollen in the peat tells us that the beds are the remains of hazel, birch and alder, and to a lesser extent of pine and oak. The thickness of these upland peat beds tells us plainly that the tree coverage here was at one time dense, and their existence at these heights clearly indicates a much higher tree-line than that of today, which in exposed places in seldom 1,000 feet.

Warmer weather is in fact found to have occurred between 7,000 and

2,000 B.C. This however was not, again, an even progression, but divided into phases by its variation. The periods were identified and named by Axel Blytt in 1876, and are known as the *Boreal*, which lasted from 6,500 B.C. to 5,200 B.C., and was dry and cool; the *Atlantic*, from then till 3,000 B.C., which was moister and warmer, and which saw the beginnings of the 'Neolithic' period of human development. A subsequent drier but still warm period, which Blytt termed the *Sub-Boreal*, ushered in the Bronze Age, and ran from 3,000 to 850 B.C. And the last phase of pre-history, (the *Sub-Atlantic*), from 850 B.C. to the start of our own era, ending about 300 A.D., was wet and cool and covered the period of the Iron Age cultures.

Blytt was working from peat deposits in Scandinavia, but his findings are broadly applicable to North Wales. Heavy rainfall in the west during the Atlantic period led to the rapid formation of peat beds. The drier, Boreal, period, had led to the establishment of birch and hazel, whereas that dampening climate favoured the dominance of alder and oak. As it became drier again between 200 and 700 B.C. the tree line lowered and the forests became less dense. This, as we shall see, had a crucial influence on the settlements of human beings.

When they first entered our area, in Neolithic times, their use of this land was restricted to a few bare coastal areas, where the sea had led to the depletion of the forest. There is no clear evidence of earlier settlements, (though isolated finds from the Middle Stone Age have been made), and our history must start there, in the warm, damp conditions of the Atlantic period, about 3,000 B.C., when the old thick forest cloaked the land and was only then beginning to succumb to heavy rainfall in the uplands.

In spite of their limited habitat the people of the New Stone Age have left us remarkable memorials of themselves, in the form of the great burial chambers which still magnificently dot our countryside. These, in North Wales usually of a simple, chamber form, occur in definite clusters in the places where one would expect early habitation to be favoured, notably the southern side of the Lleyn peninsula and the Harlech coast. It was, we may guess, the sea which made these spots habitable, and also the sea which brought their inhabitants to them.

The tombs are similar in structure to those of Ireland (where the greatest of them all, Newgrange, has now been dated to 3,200 B.C.) and show a connection too to some of southern Britain, so that we may see this area of North Wales as a half-way station between those notable sites of Neolithic activity. Our tombs are mainly of the 'portal' type, named after their most characteristic feature, a pair of upright stones with a flat one across the top of them forming the capstone of the chamber itself. The apparent portal was not, however, used as a doorway, since it was invariably blocked by another stone laid across the gap between the uprights, and in any case the whole thing was designed to be covered over. Its shape must therefore be symbolic, but the message still eludes us.

Occasional tombs occur inland, but still in connection with waterways, as at Maen y Bardd and Capel Garmon in the Conwy valley. The great majority, however, lie near the coast. There are no less than twenty west of the Conwy on the mainland, and Anglesey boasts a further twenty more, with indications that many have been lost. This gives Anglesey, in fact, the greatest concentration of megalithic evidence in Britain. The fact that Ireland is supreme in this respect points to a cultural as well as a geographical link between Anglesey and Ireland at this early time.

To see what the tombs would originally have looked like, one should go to Bryn Celli Ddu, near Llanddaniel Fab in Anglesey, since this has its mound in place, or rather replaced. There would in fact have been more of this, as is indicated by the outer circle of stones. Another tomb in recognisably good condition, but without the covering mound, is the one at Capel Garmon near Betws-y-coed, which has the added advantage of a splendid setting. For sheer power of impact, on a rocky hillside overlooking the Conwy valley, it would be hard to beat Maen y Bardd, alongside the Roman road above Ro-wen. Although reduced to little more than a massive capstone on the points of a handful of uprights, it juts with a sense of confidence and defiance, as if its makers knew that it would prove to be indestructible.

Indeed that is about the only thing we know of them, that they built these things to last. We do not know why they built them, or why they built them where they did. It is after all an easy matter to dispose of the dead, and this was far from being an easy course. We know that it must have been important to them to do things this way, since the efforts involved would have been considerable. We do also know that they had the power to do it, and therefore the degree of organisation required to undertake what amount to large-scale civil engineering works for a small population.

In view of this proven ability we may attribute the erection of at least some of the standing stones and stone circles to them as well. Where these have been dated elsewhere they are found to have originated in the late Stone Age, that is before about 2,300 B.C. Stonehenge itself, which has been extensively dated, was constructed in phases over a period of more than a thousand years, spanning the transition from the late Stone Age to the Bronze Age, the first phase now being dated to around 3,135 B.C. Unlike the chambered tombs the stone circles in North Wales do not mainly lie on the coast (although those on Holy island are inevitably not far from the sea) but rather in upland areas, which may indicate a slightly later date for them than for the cromlechs, perhaps even that of the Bronze Age, by which time the forest was thinning at its upper level.

The finest circle of standing stones in North Wales, though small in comparison to the greater ones of Britain, is undoubtedly that known anomalously as the Druids' Circle, above Penmaenmawr. Here there are ten stones still standing, of a likely circle of more than twelve, with numerous associated formations nearby. Indeed across the whole of the mountain moorland where the Druids' Circle stands there are some six lesser circles and about the same number of independent standing stones.

Once again we cannot fail to be impressed by these people's determination. These single stones are massive, and even with modern equipment it would be a challenge to position them on end in such a way that they would stay there for at least four thousand years. The two tall stones at Penrhos Feilw, near Holyhead, have a special elegance about them, but once again, for setting and atmospheric power the two which give the pass of Bwlch y Ddeufaen its name, the pass of the two stones, have a clear advantage. Standing either side of the Roman road as it crosses the moorland in its journey from the Conwy valley to the coast, they loom impressively in the upland air.

Usually in pairs, one round and bulky and one more sharply faced, the first with a round blunt top and the second slanting to a point, the stones implore us to understand them. That they must have had some significance to those who erected them we naturally assume (although there are those who claim prosaicly that they were put there for cattle to rub on), yet all we can actually know of them is that they are where they are. The position of them, as those at Bwlch y Ddeufaen, is such that they could be marking a route, though since in that case the track crosses a narrow pass between two great mountains at this point there would seem to be little need for that. Some are in any case set apparently arbitrarily on the featureless slopes of mountains. Yet no-one would go to the trouble of putting up such a weighty item without taking some care in its siting, so that even these spots must be significant in some way.

In the case of the stone circles several things are known. Many years of careful inspection by various archeologists failed to identify a comprehensive alignment of stone circles with sunrises or sunsets. Some pointed one way, some another. The famous heel-stone of Stonehenge, over which the midsummer sun rises, had misled them into trying to expand this connection into a general law. Instead it has been more credibly claimed that the alignment of some of the circles is related not to the sun but to the moon.

The standing stones might then as well have had an astronomical function. In any case any gnomon is potentially a clock. We must see them as occurring along with the development of agriculture, and for settled farmers, as opposed to travelling herdsmen, a reliable knowledge of the passage of the seasons would be important. You have to know, for instance, when you are half-way through the winter season, so that you can ration your reserves. You have to know in advance when the spring will come, so that you can prepare the ground for planting. Moreover if it is the case, as farmers and gardeners have always maintained, that seeds germinate best if sown early in the cycle of the moon, a knowledge of lunar timing would be useful and therefore give one a competitive advantage.

Since it has been shown that stone circles were built in Britain over the course of two thousand years, and since the earlier ones are said to be more accurately aligned to the heavenly bodies than those built late, it is quite likely that the building of them simply became a tradition, the purpose of which had been long forgotten. Perhaps by then other ways of determining the calendar, for instance by counting days, had been arrived at. For one reason or another stone circle building died out by 1,200 B.C. Over such a long period of time it is likely, of course, that the stone circles, and to a lesser extent the standing stones, developed a number of functions, whatever their original one might have been. They would provide a focal point for the community, and a site for markets, meetings, celebrations or even just entertainments.

Although no sign of settlements can be traced for this period, and indeed the finding of human and animal bones from the New Stone Age in a cave on the Great Orme gives some support to the idea that these people were cave dwellers, there is remarkable testimony here to their technological development. Before the knowledge of the use of metal, stone was an important commodity, and North Wales was one of Britain's prime producers of stone tools.

The Craig Llwyd axe factory at Penmaenmawr has now unfortunately gone the way of the hill-fort there, engulfed in the all-devouring quarry. It is of course the quality of Penmaenmawr's stone which gave rise to both, so that in a sense the quarry is simply the distant descendant of the axe factory. Craig Llwyd is of particular interest because it implies trade, and hence the social and political structures necessary to maintain that. Actually the Craig Llwyd complex is better referred to as an industrial area rather than a factory, since it stretches over more than two miles and contains three separate sites of activity. It is clear that a well-organised and highly-productive force was at work, producing both light axes for their own use and heavier ones for forest clearance elsewhere. They were exploiting their skills as manufacturers and their area's valuable raw material.

Penmaenmawr stone is so easily identifiable by microscopic inspection that the spread of Craig Llwyd products can be confidently defined. These have been found all over North Wales, but their distribution is much wider than that. They have been found in mid and south Wales too, and throughout the west of England, where they occur in clusters at the heads of rivers such as the Severn and Avon, as if borne there by water. They occur in northern England too, on rivers again, and one example lies as far north as the Firth of Forth. In southern England they are found along the coast, at the tip of Cornwall and around the Solent; and again they cluster at the head of the river complex which reaches to Salisbury Plain. Two axes from Craig Llwyd have even been found in Northern Ireland.

The evidence on the site itself is mainly in the form of waste material, flakes from the carving of axes and a number of broken finished products. It is thought from the nature of these that the process involved several stages. The material was cut from the rock-face and from scree, and rough-formed into blocks. These were then flaked into shape by hammers made of beach stones. The axes, by then of the required shape, were taken to a different site to be ground and polished.

All this went on for probably several hundred years around or before 2,500 B.C. It is now known that as early as 2,000 B.C. (much earlier than had previously been thought) the human world of North Wales began to change. Discovery of the use of metal led to a new technology and a new way of life. Before we take a close look at the effects of this, it would be interesting to consider the causes.

It has long been assumed that the use of metal originated on the continent and spread from there to Britain. This is because of the relative dating of the mine workings there and here, and it has been largely overturned by pioneering work in the Great Orme copper mines. It would be impossible to overstate the importance of this discovery, which has revolutionised our understanding of prehistory. It is tempting to see it, in fact, as evidence that the movement of influence went the other way, from innovation in Britain outwards to the continent. However such a new way of life as is indicated not only by the facilitating use of metal but by such things as burial customs, indicating different religious beliefs, points to the possibility of a movement into our area of a new group of people. Bone shapes also indicate that about 2,600 B.C. a wave of newcomers entered Britain, with rounder skulls than those of the original natives, and thus it may have been they who brought with them the first use of metal.

We have already seen how changes in climate could lead to the movements of people: such changes could both enable this (as by the end of glaciation or the depletion of forest) or induce it, as by increasingly bad conditions or by drought. The warmer and drier times which coincided with the beginning of the Bronze Age in western Britain made this area more attractive to a technologically advanced people, who could clear the thinning forests to a lower height and till the land. At the same time elsewhere increasing warmth and dryness led to the migration of pastoral people out of the semi-desert areas, leading to pressure on the intermediate zone. Pressure from one side leads in due course to a wave of expansion on the other, so that in the course of time the drying of wells in Central Asia could bring about the end of the Stone Age in North Wales.

From around 2,000 B.C. the forest edge became lower, and settlements above the tree level were now possible in the upper valleys. We may in fact see one of them in the valley falling from Llyn Dulyn, above the Conwy valley, where a large group of huts and compounds is similar in structure to those complexes identified as Bronze Age elsewhere, for instance on Dartmoor. If this is so we can see how farming settlements followed the valleys downwards, and in doing so, both by clearances and by the effects of grazing, themselves accelerated the fall-back of the forest.

If this complex below Dulyn does indeed represent a dwelling area of the people of this time (and this is disputed) it is more or less on its own in that capacity. We know quite a lot of other things they built, but have not yet discovered their homes. A possibly Bronze Age find inside the Iron Age ramparts of Tre'r Ceiri (in the form of a burial cairn) is not enough by itself to give us a theory that the reason is that the occupation of sites continued uninterrupted into the Iron Age, and so had become submerged by that in our dating system. We would have found considerably more Bronze Age evidence in the excavations of Iron Age sites (though admittedly these have been few in number) if this were so. However what we have in some quantity for this period is evidence of their distinctive burial forms.

The Bronze Age people cremated their dead, sometimes sealing the ashes in urns and placing the urns at the centre of a mound of stones. The mound served as multiple burial sites; one excavated at Penmaenmawr in 1889 contained no less than eleven urns and eight other cremations.

Burials usually took place on high ground, and indeed the summits of mountains were much favoured for this purpose. The summits of most of the mountains in the Carneddau range are surmounted by Bronze Age burial cairns. Indeed there are about forty burial cairns in the area of this range alone. Analysis of the height-distribution of cairn burials in the former county of Caernarfonshire shows that by far the largest proportion occurs between the 1,200 and the 1,500 contours. The number below 500 feet is relatively tiny.

The dry and warm conditions of the 'Sub-Boreal' period when these monuments were built meant that it would have been possible and convenient for their builders actually to live at this altitude. There is no sign, however, that they did so. We can only conclude that wherever they lived they made their dwellings out of destructible material, since the stone-based hut circles which are so common in North Wales have never been dated to so early a period. Perhaps again this is a function of the weather. In rougher winds you needed a stone base to your hut. In warm dry times a mere wigwam would do.

Like the burial mounds of the New Stone Age, the Bronze Age cairns are founded on a ring of stones which supports the mound itself. The latter has however in many cases overrun this ring, which is not normally visible.

The cairns are of very different sizes, varying (where they have been measured) from fifteen to sixty-two feet in diameter. In height they vary considerably, according to the degree of disturbance as well as to their original size. The largest in our area, which admittedly makes use of a natural outcrop of rock, is that on the summit of Carn Guwch, a round hill on the Lleyn peninsula, which rises to twenty feet in height.

In addition to the stone-built cairns, burials of this period were sometimes covered by earthen barrows, marked on the large-scale Ordnance Survey maps with the word 'tumulus', the distinction between these and the stone heaps being, it seems, purely to do with the availability of materials. In the western uplands stones are plentiful everywhere, and heaps can be made of them; further east the land is smoother, and here there is plenty of earth. No less than ten earthen barrows lie alongside the road crossing the uplands between Colwyn Bay and Pentrefoelas, a sign perhaps that this was an ancient trackway.

Many of these are difficult to find, but a group of three is easily identified as it lies on top of a ridge called Mwdwl Eithin, about midway between Llangernyw and Eglwysbach. One of these three is much more intact, and so more prominent, than the other two, a solid lump of turf standing against the sky; a trig point now stands incongruously on top of it. It is some nine feet high and eighty-eight yards around its circle.

The central example of these three was excavated in 1912 by Dr Willoughby Gardner, and was found to contain a stone circle surrounding a central cremation and two others, one contained in an urn, by then crushed and fragmented but still identifiable. The earth mounds have in fact much in common with the burial cairns, in size, shape and in what they contained.

The site itself of these Bronze Age mounds is also reminiscent of the locations of their contemporary cairns, as on the Carneddau and the Great Orme's Head. It is an inspiring spot. Like the setting of the (perhaps older) stone circles, as for instance Castlerigg in Cumbria, or indeed Stonehenge on Salisbury Plain, it is a place which generates an unavoidable soaring of the spirit. Its all-round outlook includes the mountains and the Conwy valley, and eastwards the long rolling stretch of Hiraethog, folded like a crumpled sheet. In any season it is potentially a bleak and windy place. Exposure goes with such an expansive view. In winter a vicious cold comes off the hills or across Hiraethog.

Bronze Age cremations have been found at the feet of the great standing stones, leading some to conclude that these are Bronze Age in origin too. It does not follow of course from this concurrence that the two are contemporary; a pre-existing monument might well have seemed a suitable location for a burial. The fact that there is also a coincidence between the forms of some burial cairns and smaller stone circles (since some of the cairns contain a circle of upright stones as well as the outer kerb) has led some to the view that the stone circles are really the skeletons of burial cairns, and so of Bronze Age date. Those which have been dated, however, show that circle-building began at least as early as 3,000 B.C.; and evidence of later Bronze Age burials in earlier circles is plentiful in Britain, the proof that it is later being the disruption or neglect of the original plan. It can be said, however, that there is probable overlap between the two forms, so that circle-building became an influence on the methods of cairn-building.

The cairns contain at their centre a small stone cell, known as a cist, which housed the main burial. This is constructed in the form of a box of stone slabs, as may be seen in the case of Barclodiad y Gawres, alongside the Roman road as it passes through Bwlch y Ddeufaen.

One other widespread feature which is sometimes ascribed to the Bronze Age is the phenomenon known as 'burnt mounds', consisting of heaps of burnt and shattered stone, always near to a source of water. These, though they are not very visible, are numerous in the same areas as the cairns. More than forty have been identified in the western uplands, between the Conwy and the coast.

Difficult to find, and quite impossible if you follow the map references given in the Ancient Monuments Commission Inventory, which are wildly astray, these are, it must be said, by no means worth the trudge through the bog. The modern Ordnance Survey maps locate them accurately, but the land is so featureless in the areas where they lie that you find them largely by luck. Sometimes grassed over, in other cases a half-ring of boulders among the reeds, they would be indistinguishable from the rest of the upland countryside were it not for their distinctive crescent shape. All they have to offer, apart from a walk in open Welsh hill country, is their undeniable air of mystery. 'Mounds of burnt stone', as the Ordnance Survey maps say. Perhaps a slight discolouration of the lower parts of some of the stones confirms this, but on the whole we have to take this designation on trust.

Not surprisingly, these have long puzzled archeologists, being apparently composed entirely of stones which have been burnt in a fire. Excavation of an example in Ireland suggests a cooking function, and indeed the mounds have traditionally been called boiling mounds. However a further investigation of an instance of these widespread phenomena in the Orkneys, in 1974, and at Bournville near Birmingham in 1987 suggest the possibility that they were bathhouses, since they contain cubicles around a central trough. Such diverse early civilisations as those of the Sioux, the Slavs and the Maya used water poured over heated stones to provide a steam-bath, very much like a sauna. Radiocarbon dated materials gives a date for the Midlands example of 1,500 B.C., which tallies approximately with dated specimens in another excavated example in County Cork.

Until quite recently our knowledge of the Bronze Age inhabitants of North Wales was mainly limited to their treatment of their dead. Now we know a great deal more about what they did while they were living.

During the 1980's the Great Orme Exploration Society, founded for the purpose, began investigating the ancient copper mines above Llandudno which fell out of use during the last century. An early radiocarbon date from a charcoal deposit fell just short of 1,000 B.C., and proved that the mines were worked before the Iron Age. This led to the expectation of finding further Bronze Age workings, which was in due course amply fulfilled. The earliest date so far established is 1,800 B.C., which significantly pushes back the previously accepted date for the start of the Bronze Age in North Wales. Before this discovery the date had been put at 900 B.C., so that the difference is radical.

The mine-workings, which opened to the public in 1991, are still being investigated and opened up. The presently accessible tunnels, which extend 300 metres into the Orme and sink to a depth, in a complex network, of some 250 feet below its surface, provide a total distance of about five miles; the scale of the whole thing, in fact, is that of a major industrial site. The shafts themselves vary greatly in size and character. Some are so small that they could only have been worked by children. Others are spacious, and one vast cavern, previously thought to have been part of the Victorian workings, has now been shown to have been in use in Bronze Age times.

The Bronze Age workers used largely bone tools to work the seams, some antlers but mainly the bones of cattle, over 8,000 of which have been found in the Orme mines. They also used stone hammers made of beach stones, particularly favouring those derived from the headland of Penmaenmawr, famous since the New Stone Age for the hardness of its stone. Over 900 of these stone tools have been found. The hard hammers and pounding stones however seem to have been relatively little used, and the widespread use of bone, and in rare cases of comparatively soft stone, argues that the rock within which lay the ore was soft and fragile.

The workers also used to crack the rock by banking fires against it, an early form of blasting. This (and the use of bone) had the unintended effect of leaving us datable evidence.

So far no evidence of a settlement nor any signs of habitations have been found, a puzzle which has confronted us on other Bronze Age sites. There must have been a lot of people here for a long time, and evidence of their lives must lie somewhere under the Orme's turf. So far also no signs of smelting sites have been identified, and in view of the very large amount of ore which must have been extracted over this considerable period, these would be evident enough in the form of large deposits of charcoal, if they existed. It is likely therefore that the ore was taken elsewhere to be smelted, presumably to some more forested area, of which there were plenty in the surrounding valleys.

Copper mining seems to have come to an end on the Great Orme (as far as this early period is concerned) about 600 B.C. Its proved survival there for more than a thousand years by then says a great deal about the stability, and social organisation, of the time. We have seen already ample evidence that it would be a gross mistake to think (as previous generations have done) of these early civilisations as primitive. As early as the New Stone Age the megalith builders were displaying highly sophisticated technical skills, as well as an elevated conceptual system underlying their use. The production of so much copper on the Orme implies a trading structure. This is not speculation. There is simply no alternative. Trading involves a developed system of exchange, and sufficiently stable political arrangements to enable the transportation of valuable commodities.

Copper itself is not much use, being too soft to make implements, tools, or weapons; it is only of importance as an element in the alloy bronze, the other ingredient of which is tin. It is probable that alloys occurred originally accidentally, and other minerals such as lead can combine with copper to produce an improved metal. The point about the Bronze Age which seems of greatest interest, but which has not been adequately addressed, is that copper and tin do not occur together, so that the one has to be taken to the other. There are no large deposits of tin in Wales and the nearest tin mines are in Cornwall, where there is an abundance of it. Another puzzle, however, is that tin was not mined in prehistoric times, so that one wonders how they managed to make bronze. The answer, it seems, is that at that time there was alluvial tin (a possibility which is indicated by an early reference to a trade in 'river tin') of which, in the nature of things, there would be no evidence now. If there was (for instance) tin in the silt of the Conwy river, it would make sense for the smelting to take place on its bank.

In any case the amount of copper mined points to an intentional surplus of metal goods produced, and so to organised trading. This in turn implies a high degree of social, political and economic organisation, and the fact that we do not normally associate these qualities with people who lived nearly 3,000 years ago is a measure of our ignorance, not of theirs. The unavoidable impact of the Great Orme Bronze Age copper mines is that they make us humble.

Bibliography

British Regional Geography: North Wales. Bernard Smith, revised T. Neville George. HMSO.
The Ice Age in Cwm Idwal and *The Ice Age in Y Glyderau and Nant Ffrancon*. Kenneth Addison, 10 Hurst Close, Borselly, Shropshire.
British Landscape Through Maps: Snowdonia. C. Embleton. The Geographical Association.
'The Climate of Pre-Historic Britain'. C.E.P. Books. *Antiquity* December 1972, Vol.1. No.IV. p.42.
'Climate and Migration'. J.C. Curry. *Antiquity* September 1928. Vol.11 No.VII. p.292.
Royal Commission on Ancient Monuments Inventories: *Anglesey* and *Caernarvonshire*. HMSO.
'Rings of Stone', Aubrey Burl. Weidenfeld and Nicholson. See also *Antiquity* December 1980. No.54. p.p.191-198.
'Early Mining at the Great Orme's Head: Some Observations and Implications'. C.A. Lewis. Unpublished paper.
The author also wishes to thank Tony Hammond, of the Great Orme Mines Ltd., for his insights and information.

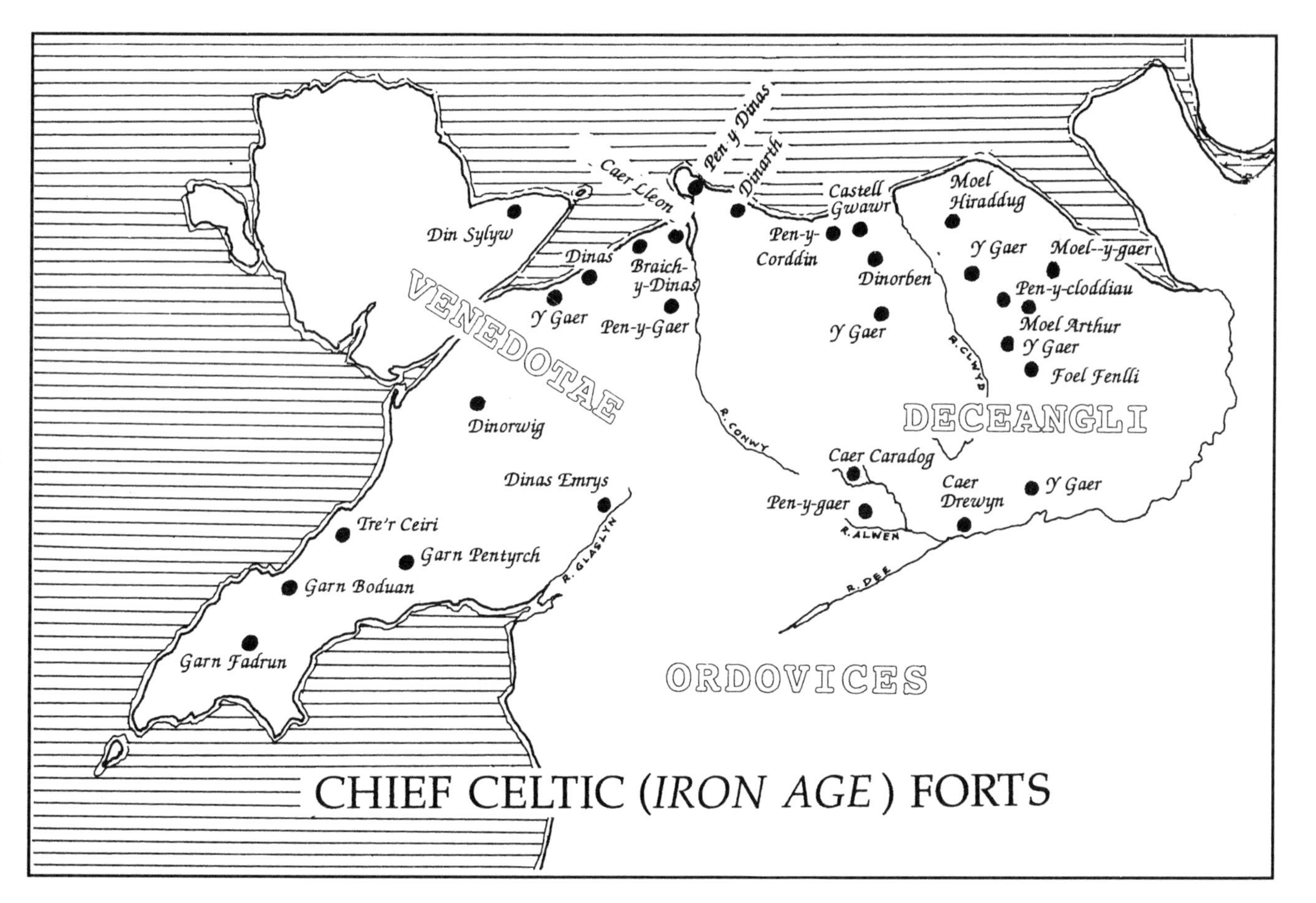

Pen y Dinas
Caer Lleon
Dinarth
Castell Gwawr
Moel Hiraddug
Din Sylyw
Pen-y-Corddin
Y Gaer
Moel--y-gaer
Dinas
Braich-y-Dinas
Dinorben
Pen-y-cloddiau
VENEDOTAE
Y Gaer
Pen-y-Gaer
Y Gaer
Moel Arthur
Y Gaer
R. CLWYD
Foel Fenlli
Dinorwig
DECEANGLI
R. CONWY
Caer Caradog
Dinas Emrys
Caer Drewyn
Y Gaer
Pen-y-gaer
Tre'r Ceiri
R. ALWEN
Garn Pentyrch
R. GLASLYN
Garn Boduan
R. DEE
Garn Fadrun
ORDOVICES
CHIEF CELTIC (IRON AGE) FORTS

Step Change

The classification of human social history into 'Ages', based on the materials used, was first proposed by C.J. Thomsen in 1836. It has its uses, but must increasingly be modified by qualification. Iron, for instance, was in use long before any time one could identify as an Iron *age*. We should not think of hard cut-off points; the diffusion of new ideas and techniques is likely to have taken rather more the form of a tidal creep, each wave pushing ahead of it the previous one.

Iron does not occur in natural form on earth, (except in Greenland, where it has been disgorged by eruptions), and must therefore normally be smelted from its ore. It does however occur abundantly in meteorites, and it can be shown by analysis that these formed the first source of worked iron. Iron objects have been found in Egypt from an early date, for instance beads from about 3,500 B.C. The first instances of smelting iron occur during the Bronze Age, both in Mesopotamia and in Egypt, where meteoric iron had been used for ritualistic purposes from early times.

There are records of the use of iron for blades of daggers in Egypt before 1,350 B.C., and at about that date we have the best record of all in the form of the iron-bladed dagger found in the tomb of Tutankamun. The use of iron then spread fast through Syria and Palestine during the last centuries of the second millennium B.C.

We must therefore not think of the coming of the Iron Age as being anything to do with a sudden invention occurring in Europe at about that time; clearly the knowledge of the technique is more likely to have spread there from Asia Minor. It is traditionally supposed that the change in way of life which is indicated by the artefacts was due to the arrival of new groups of people with superior tools and weapons. We know that something similar happened elsewhere, for instance in northern Syria, where iron-using people destroyed a Bronze Age city, and thus ended the Bronze Age there, at the end of the 13th century B.C. The idea of migrations, 'waves of invaders', is now academically out of fashion, some scholars now preferring to think of the process as a development and spread of ideas. This trend itself may however give rise to over-generalisation. We must at least consider the possibility (encouraged to some extent by archeology) that in Britain, and specifically in North Wales, the Bronze Age was brought to an end by the arrival of new people bearing new skills.

If that is what happened, who were these people?

It has been found convenient from at least the 16th century, in Britain, to call them the Celts. It is not at all certain that the people referred to ever thought of themselves as a cohesive group, let alone that they even called themselves Celts. Indeed the use of the term 'Celts' to cover the diverse groups of people living in Britain and Europe at the time of the expansion of the Roman Empire, and hence to describe their descendants today, is based on a series of old but clearly identifiable mistakes.

Herodotus, a Greek historian of the mid-5th century B.C., is our first source; other classical writers followed his terminology. He mentions the Celts in connection with the source of the Danube, and in doing so perhaps implies that his transcription of their name, *Keltoi,* is what he understood them to have called themselves. This suggestion has some support, much later, from Julius Caesar.

A little earlier than Caesar, in the same century, the first century B.C., a Greek writer and philosopher called Posidonius wrote a 'History' which we know of only through slightly later Greek authors, Diodurus Siculus and particularly Strabo, who cites him extensively. From these references we know that Posidonius dealt with the 'Celts' in some detail. He is important too as an influence on Caesar, who plagiarises and occasionally varies his account.

It seems that Posidonius' original descriptions were based on first-hand experience, since he had lived in Gaul. He depicts a people with firmly defined habits and a way of life which is, to him, curious because quite un-Latin. ('They do not use olive oil because of its scarcity, and because of its unfamiliarity it appears unpleasant to them.') They had an odd mixture of civilised habits, such as formal dining, with primitive customs, such as severing their enemies heads and keeping them as souvenirs in a chest. One characteristic which he notes we may find familiar, though this is hardly proof that these people he calls the Celts were in fact, as is assumed, the ancestors of the Welsh. They had a marked tendency to burst into song.

It is Julius Caesar, in *'De Bello Gallico'*, his memoirs of the 50's B.C., who gives us our main reason for identifying the Celts with the Gauls. He says explicitly that they are called *'Celtae'* in their own language, but *'Galli'* in Latin. He also rather inconsistently distinguishes these 'Gauls' from the other people living in 'Gaul', the Belgae and the Aquitani. These three groups, he says, have different languages, traditions and laws. If he is right, then there were three main groups of people living in the area he called Gaul, and they were distinct, the Celts being only one of them. It definitely does not seem from this that the Celts were a related group of nations, rather than one tribe in such a group, and when we come to the descriptions of Britain, a short time later, and its relation to Gaul, there is no suggestion of Britain's being Celtic. Indeed one writer of the period (Strabo) explicitly contrasts the people of Britain with the Celts, and Caesar himself says that the coast of Britain was colonised by the Belgae, whom he has previously distinguished from the Celts, while the inland part was inhabited by people who regarded themselves as indigenous. A little later (the first century A.D.) Tacitus tells us that 'the peoples nearest to the Gauls are correspondingly like them . . . ' so that 'we may believe that it was the Gauls who took possession of the neighbouring island . . . There is no great difference in language' – indicating, however, that there is *some* difference.

We can of course argue backwards from the existing languages towards their classical European forebears to make the connection between the inhabitants of Britain and those of Gaul, and as we shall see the artwork on artefacts from this period also relates the pre-Roman population of Britain to the continental people we have become accustomed to calling Celtic.

Our own confusion, in fact, in our use of the term 'Celts', is mirrored by that of the classical authors, from whom it is in any case derived. Diodurus Siculus, a historian of the period succeeding Caesar, to some extent follows him, but is more specific: the Celts lived between the Alps and the Pyrenees; the Gauls lived north of them; the Romans, he says, mistakenly lumped the two together. Strabo, like Diodurus writing in Greek, around the turn of the era, makes a further point about this possible mistake: the Greeks called all the inhabitants of the area Keltoi, because of the prominence of the one group of them, the Celtae.

Although the people we are considering may then not have known themselves by one name, it is a visible fact that they had several things in common. These relating characteristics can be considered under three heads: their language, their artwork, and their religion.

Let us briefly see how much we know about these three, since they are all relevant to an understanding of the scene in North Wales prior to the coming of the Romans.

First, the language. Our early sources show that Gaulish personal and tribal names are related to the modern group of languages known (since the work done by George Buchanan during the 17th century) as Celtic. Edward Llwyd, at the end of the 17th century, also did much pioneer work in classifying these, from which it became clear that the correlation points to an original language group, and hence by inference to a related group of peoples who spoke those languages. Inscriptions and coins found in the areas supposedly occupied by the Celts further support this hypothesis with hard archeological evidence, and the residue of Celtic place-names in these same areas provides further backing. From this it can be seen that a group of related languages formed part of the reality of ancient Europe, and although we have seen that the term 'Celtic' is very probably the wrong one to use to describe this group, it is the one which has been used since the 16th century and is so commonly understood that we are undoubtedly stuck with it.

The fact that the Celtic languages which were once spoken over much of Europe only remain in very small pockets is due to the wholesale domination of Europe by the Romans and then the Germanic tribes, the latter in the 5th century A.D. It is clear from the classical writers that during the Roman occupation and its aftermath it was considered smart to speak Latin, while a Celtic language still remained the general one. It would be interesting, but outside our present purpose, to investigate the reasons the European countries eventually adopted the languages they did – why, for instance, did France, invaded (as Gaul) by Germanic tribes, the Franks, end up speaking a Latin language? Here however we are concerned with tracing the roots of the people of North Wales, whose language has achieved a remarkable survival. It is remarkable that it is Britain, in fact, not Gaul, which has retained the surviving Celtic tongues. (Breton even was a later import from here.)

Without wishing to denigrate the brave survivals of Irish and Scottish Gaelic, or to fail to mourn the virtual demise of Cornish, Cumbrian and Manx, it must be said that it is only in Wales, and most noticeably in parts of North Wales, that this once great family of languages is represented by a healthy living descendant. That this is no mere achievement of preservation, suited to a museum, or in this case a reservation, but the real medium of day to day activity, is not always appreciated by outsiders.

The survival of anything is a cause for celebration, but that such a valuable residue of our pan-European background remains intact, alive and well and in North Wales, should give us special pleasure. Language is the natural medium of cultural identity, and this symptom of the distinctiveness of Wales is an important resource contributing to the rich texture of variety which characterises the island of Britain.

Turning now to the other common features relating the pre-Roman inhabitants of continental Europe to those of Britain, we find, in both the archeological discoveries and the continuing tradition, a marked artistic style which we may as well follow the custom and call Celtic. It is curvilinear, much given to swirls and loops. It occurs not only on ornaments and domestic items, but on shields and warriors' helmets. It is found in Germany, France, Italy and Holland, from the 4th century B.C. onwards, and in large quantities all over England.

In North Wales a hoard of some ninety objects was found in 1943 in a marshy area (near the creek which separates Holy Island from the rest of Anglesey), known as Llyn Cerrig Bach. Peat was being extracted from the area for spreading somewhere else in Anglesey, in connection with some Government war-time scheme. A strong iron chain got caught in the teeth of a harrow, and was then put to use behind the tractor to tow out of the marsh lorries which had got stuck. Nobody realised at the time that this useful item was 2,000 years old. Only when other metal objects and numerous animal bones appeared did the Clerk of Works inform the National Museum.

The Llyn Cerrig Bach find is one of the most important, and most puzzling, sources of information about the Iron Age population of North Wales. What is at once striking about the objects found is how diverse they are; there is no consistency about them which would help to explain their deposition. Many of them are in good condition, so that we may assume that they were not being discarded as broken or worn out. This is then no rubbish heap. Indeed their high quality is striking, and this together with their variety and the presence also of numerous animal bones suggests a sacrificial offering. It is known that the Celtic people of Europe did throw objects of value into rivers and lakes – hence the old custom of casting coins into wells and fountains in the hopes of gaining good fortune – presumably as votive offerings, and the items found at Llyn Cerrig Bach are consistent with the sacrifice of a good specimen of each type and category of possession.

There are weapons: two-edged swords, the style of which relates them to Celtic swords in continental Europe and suggests a 1st century B.C. date; spears, or rather spear-heads, some over two feet long, with sockets into which would be fitted the traditional ash-wood shafts. Parts of vehicles such as iron tyres, and bands apparently from the hubs of wheels, indicating the use of chariots, which it is known from Caesar the people of Britain used in warfare, in conjunction with thrown javelins:

> When fighting with chariots the Britons start by driving all over the field throwing javelins, usually with the result that the fear inspired by the horses and the noise of the wheels are enough to create disorder in their opponents' ranks.

They are, he recognises, great horsemen:

> . . . by daily training and practice they attain such skill that even on a steep slope they can control the horses at full gallop, and stop them short in a moment.

And sure enough at Llyn Cerrig Bach we find horse harness and tackle in abundance, mainly two- and three-link bridle bits. These bits are remarkably reminiscent of such things still in use today. They are finely made, and with an eye on aesthetic appeal. It has been calculated that they were used on small ponies, no more than $10^1/_2$ hands, similar, in fact, to the Welsh mountain ponies of today.

It is not too fanciful in fact to relate these North Wales Celts, on the evidence of this find, to Caesar's description of Britons further south. Bridle-bits similar to those found at Llyn Cerrig Bach have been discovered all over Britain. A close study of the Anglesey ones relates them to examples from the Mendips, to such an extent that it is conjectured that they actually came from there.

A certain militancy is also attested by the two well-preserved gang chains, consisting of five neck-rings joined by figure-of-eight links to form a series of constraints about two feet apart, which imply the presence of prisoners. Once again the chains are very finely made, and their construction displays both craftsmanship and technology.

So far the finds show us a military culture. We get a hint of a formidable fighting force. But Llyn Cerrig Bach has other things to tell us too.

Currency bars suggest a trading nation, bars of iron being of value and perhaps exchanged for produce. A sickle points to farming, and we are in an area of fertile soil. Part of a bronze trumpet suggests an element of ritual, and its similarity to trumpets found in Ireland suggests a common culture, if not more direct influence. A bronze coil which was thought to have decorated a staff also suggests ritual. Perhaps the most famous and fascinating find is a plaque ornamented with a complicated pattern of crescents and leaf-like bosses. Highly artistic in style it speaks of both display and refinement, though its exact use remains a mystery. The hole forming the centre of its upper part suggests a costume use, but as the circle is closed it could not have fitted round a neck.

The objects found at Llyn Cerrig Bach all date (where dating is possible) from the first and second centuries B.C. They come from diverse places, probably from north-east Ireland, south-west, eastern and south-east England, suggesting that Anglesey was on a trade route rather than that it was itself a manufacturing centre. Close links with Ireland are later echoed in the mythology, particularly in the story of Branwen, itself set in Anglesey, and this traditional tale may have its roots in this early period. Several of the early hut circles, such as those on nearby Holy Island, are known as 'Cytiau Gwyddelod', the Irishmen's huts. We shall be wondering again whether these clues and others give us reason to think of Anglesey as a place colonised from Ireland. The Llyn Cerrig Bach find is not definite evidence for this, but at least it points to a closely-knit group of people, perhaps almost a homogeneous nation, covering the British Isles as a whole.

The dating of the artefacts and their character are consistent with this collection being a sacrifice made on the arrival of the Romans, in 61 A.D., so that this is often assumed to be the explanation. The find is consistent, in fact, with the sort of mixture of militancy and priesthood which (as we shall shortly see) the Romans described as being the sort of population they found there.

Turning finally to the religion of the ancient Celts we may likewise point to possible survivals of old themes in modern North Wales. Not that Druidism itself has survived, except in a highly fanciful resurrected form; its religious attitudes however were a product of the social and political customs of the original Celts, and this same relationship holds between the social and the religious orders of life in North Wales today.

First, though, what do we know of the religion of the original Celts? Inevitably it comes to us with some distortion, since it is not recorded by the Celts or Gauls themselves but by their enemies the Romans. Caesar tells us explicitly that the Druids forbade written records, believing oral wisdom to be more secure, and wishing to maintain their position as guardians of it:

> The Druids believe that their religion forbids them to commit their teachings to writing, although for most other purposes, such as public and private accounts, the Gauls use the Greek alphabet. But I imagine that this rule was originally established for other reasons – because they did not want their doctrine to become public property, and in order to prevent their pupils from relying on the written word and neglecting to train their memories.

As a result it is from the Roman writers, and from what we can glean from later sources, that we know of the belief-system of the ancestors of the Welsh.

Caesar particularly tells us that the Druids taught the rebirth of the soul, a belief which may have a distant reflection in the several instances in Welsh mythology in which an individual changes form, being reborn in animal or bird nature and even sometimes as someone else. This belief is of course common to several other religions, but the emphasis on the theme in mythology is particularly distinct in Wales.

Though venerated for their religious teaching the Druids were not restricted to a priestly role. They also operated the system of social and political justice. They were, in fact, a court of law. Caesar also emphasises that they were teachers and concerned with the nature of the our cosmic and terrestrial surroundings. We have other classical sources, and indeed Caesar himself may have been influenced by the work of Posidonius, but this first-hand account is probably as near as we are going to get to a view of the religion which became so important an element in the pre-Roman life of North Wales.

Caesar also records something of the background social order in which this priesthood held its position of domination. A multiple, tribal system ran through Gaulish society, and therefore doubtless through the one we are considering, in which each group was presided over by respected leaders who decided their immediate politics:

> The object of this ancient custom seems to have been to ensure that all common people should have protection against the strong: for each leader sees that no one gets the better of his supporters by force or by cunning . . .

We catch, perhaps, a glimpse of a society in which immediate power is widely disseminated and counterbalanced.

A long time later the arrival of Christianity reveals a possible parallel between Celtic and other social forms. The Celtic church originated and developed as a distinct system, often contrasted with the centralised church of Rome, that official, because Papal, body which presided over Christianity in Europe in the aftermath of the Roman empire. This is not the place to go into the differences in depth, though the subject is a fascinating one, but it may be briefly said that the Celtic church laid more emphasis on personal will and responsibility, less on centralised hierarchical authority. This dichotomy came to a head in the persons of Augustine of Hippo, writer of the 'Confessions' and 'The City of God', a father of the Roman church; and Pelagius, a British Christian, who went to Rome during the time of Augustine, the late 4th century.

Pelagius, true to his background, held that we are free to use our own efforts to achieve our own salvation. Augustine maintained that everything is pre-ordained. Pelagius found this incompatible with the notion of responsibility. This sounds much like common sense today, but at the time was condemned as heresy.

1 *The river Conwy flows past the walls of the medieval town.*

2 *Old rocks on Snowdon – Clogwyn Du'r Arddu – show the buckling and tilting caused by ancient movement of the earth's crust.*

3 *The layers of deposited limestone can be clearly seen in the Great Orme headland.*

4 *The burial chamber of Bryn Celli-ddu, on Anglesey, with its mound in place, shows us how they would have originally looked.*

5 *The Capel Garmon cromlech las lost its mound, but is otherwise in good condition.*

6 *The 'Druids' Circle' above Penmaenmawr is the best of our stone circles.*

7 8 9

The standing stones, such as these at Penrhos Feilw in Anglesey (left), at Bwlch y Ddeufaen above the Conwy valley (centre), and at Llanerch-y-medd, Anglesey (right), may well date from the same stone age period as the stone circles.

10 *As well as the stone cairns, Bronze Age burials occur also as earth barrows, such as this example on Mwdwl Eithin near Llangernyw.*

11 *Tre'r Ceiri, in Llŷn, is the best preserved example of our Iron Age hillforts.*

12 *From the Bronze Age right through the Iron Age people lived in thatched round huts based on a circle of stones.*

13 *Pen y Gaer in the Conwy valley, is a fine example of the hilltop outlooks favoured by the Iron Age builders of these forts.*

14

15

Many lesser forts appear to contribute to a possible chain, as these at Dinas above Llanfairfechan, and Caer Bach above the Conwy valley.

16 *Within the walls of Tre'r Ceiri many of the huts are still basically intact.*

17 *The ramparts of Foel Fenlli look down over Dyffryn Clwyd.*

18 *The Romans were impressed by the skill with which the British Celts handled their light chariots, one of which has been reconstructed from archeological finds.*

19 *Among the fine work found at Llyn Cerrig bach this ornamented plaque, perhaps an item of costume, stands out.*

20 *The outline of the Roman fort at Caerhun,* Canovium, *can be seen, from the air, extending from the site of the present church.*

21 *Lesser forts, such as this of Caer Gai near Bala, defended the main routes through the hills.*

22 *Fragments of Roman walling remain at Caer Llugwy.*

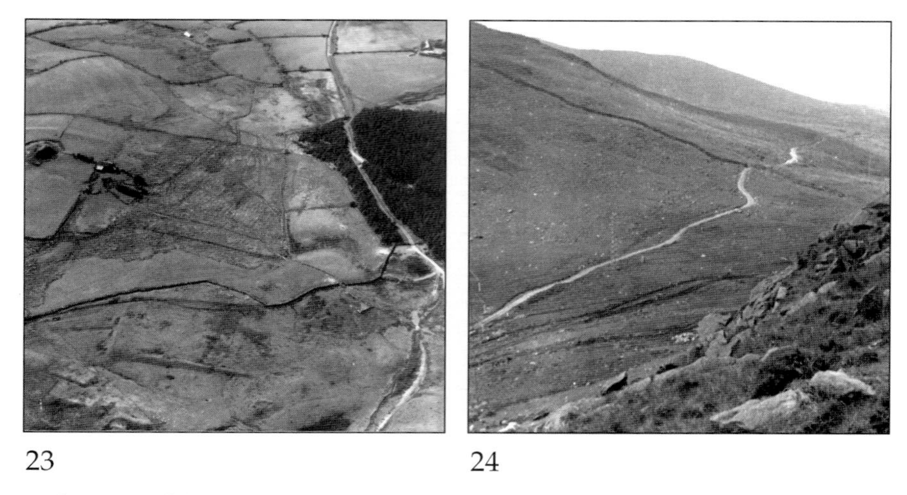

23 24

The routes of the great Roman roads can still be seen in the stretches where they cross the moors, such as at Tomen y Mur (23) and between the Conwy valley and Aber (24).

25 *Roman Segontium lies on the edge of the present town of Caernarfon.*

26 *Coins of the reign of the usurper Magnus Maximus show us the face of the original of the hero Macsen.*

27 *Coins depicting the empress Helena, perhaps the original of the heroine Elen in the Mabinogion tale of Macsen, have also been found at Caernarfon.*

28 *Dinas Emrys was the site of a prosperous court in the 'Dark Age' period.*

29 *The Vardre, above Deganwy, was the seat of Maelgwn Gwynedd in the 6th century.*

30 *Puffin Island (Ynys Seiriol), seen here from Penmon Point, had both religious and historical connections.*

31 *Old religious ruins still stand where St Seiriol set up his church on the island.*

32 *Bardsey Island (Ynys Enlli) too was a refuge for Christians.*

33 *Penmon Priory, founded by St Seiriol in the 6th century, expanded considerably in the 13th century, from which period most of its present buildings date.*

34 *Like St Seiriol at Penmon, St Cybi of Holyhead also founded a religious community in the 6th century, and these ruins surround the traditional site of his well at Llangybi, Llŷn.*

35 *One of St Beuno's foundations was the church of Clynnog Fawr, which later formed a fort on the pilgrim route to Bardsey.*

36 *Offa's Dyke is still visible for a considerable amount of its route.*

37 *Wat's dyke, the forerunner of Offa's, can be seen in fewer places, but is clear here where it skirts the ring-fort at Oswestry.*

38 *Although the stone-built churches, as that at Penmon, date from the 12th century, the religious settlements from which they developed were founded as early as the 6th.*

The point about introducing this subject here is that Augustine's followers accused Pelagius of trying to bring back Druidism. Pelagius perhaps owed his success in gaining support in Britain to the same social attitudes as had at one time favoured Druidism: the tendency to favour a personal, as against a hierarchical basis for authority, and to treat religion as a part of social life rather than a form imposed on it from elsewhere.

If this suggestion is correct it could then help to explain a strong North Wales characteristic which we shall encounter later, not only in religious forms but most prominently there: the impetus to Non-Conformism, both with and without its capital letters. Tudor reforms, such as the introduction of a more generally accountable legal system, perhaps owed something to a background awareness of the principles of the Celtic church, the history of which may go back to the very beginnings of social life in North Wales.

Whatever these long-term effects, the strength of the Druid religion in North Wales had a more immediate, and well attested, impact. Caesar tells us that Druidism in Gaul was thought to have been invented in Britain and to have been transferred to Gaul from there:

in Britannia reperta atque inde in Galliam translata existimatur

Pliny is probably wrong in viewing the influence as having gone the other way. Although Pliny's description of Druidism is a detailed one, his disagreement with Caesar on this point weakens his evidence, since Caesar drew his knowledge from first-hand accounts in Gaul. He adds that many people from Gaul still went to Britain if they wished to gain a fuller knowledge of the Druidic system.

Because it was not a literate system Druidism has left no native records, and we have in fact no evidence that it existed in Britain apart from the testimony of the classical authors, and in particular the later statement by Tacitus that it was alive and well in the first century A.D. He specifically locates its main occurrence in North Wales. When Suetonius Paulinus was governor of Britain he had a period of success in quelling the resistance to Roman rule. The island of Anglesey, however, was a problem. It was the source of a resistance movement. He then indicates why: it was a main seat of the native religion.

The destruction of the religion appears to have been a large part of Suetonius' purpose in invading Anglesey. In this explanation of the penetration of the Roman forces so far into North Wales we have the only specific mention of the Druids in Britain, so that really all we know of British Druidism is it occurred in Anglesey. Sir John Rhys, in fact, concludes that Druidism was not a British religion at all, but an Irish one, on the supposition that Anglesey was at that time an Irish colony. This however would involve believing that 'Brittania' in Caesar's statement was a mistake, and on the whole we have no cause to doubt Caesar's care and correctness.

Turning now from this scant evidence as to the early population of North Wales as found in literary sources, we may see for ourselves today the evidence on the ground, for what the Romans found when they came. The quantity of sizeable hillforts of the Iron Age period indicates a densely populated area. There are, for instance, ten within fifteen miles of each other in the area between the river Conwy and the north-west coast alone, and fifty-five altogether in the area of the old county of Caernarfonshire, forty-five of which are still in reasonably good condition.

On the whole finds from the hillforts have been disappointing, although several of them have been excavated. Dating them is consequently a rather vague procedure. From what evidence there is it may be said that at least some of the forts ceased to be occupied at about the time of the Roman invasion, while some, as discussed below, continued in use into Roman times. We may therefore think of them as being in use in general in the period immediately before the coming of Rome, that is in the hundred years or so spanning the turn of the era.

Anyone wishing to see for themselves today the impressive remains left by North Wales' Iron Age residents, should certainly undertake the steep ascent to Tre'r Ceiri, one of the largest and the best preserved of all these forts. The path leaves from near the village of Llanaelhaearn and rises to the summit of Yr Eifl, which is entirely surrounded by Tre'r Ceiri's magnificent wall. Huts and compounds cluster together all over the summit in a remarkable beehive effect. A superb view is another reward for the effort involved in rising to 1,500 feet.

Tre'r Ceiri is the showpiece of the North Wales Iron Age hillforts, but those wishing for an easier ascent might prefer to consider Pen y Gaer. This, a round hill set above the Conwy valley, is easily approached from a parking ground on its shoulder, reached by the lane rising through Llanbedr-y-cennin and then branching left. Pen y Gaer lacks Tre'r Ceiri's extensive hut systems, being much less apparently a place of habitations, but it shares with it a superb view, in this case a map-like overview of the Conwy valley. It is a fine example of a double-rampart fort, a stone-built inner wall augmented by a large bank and ditch which many archeologists conclude was added later and indicates a second phase of occupation. It also has, uniquely in England and Wales, a *'chevaux de Frise'*, an area of upright spiked stones in front of its entrance, designed to prevent a rushed assault.

These are among the highlights, the stars, of North Wales' Iron Age forts. To balance the record we should cast a glance at some lesser, and so, neglected, bit-part players in this apparently grand drama, those back-up posts which perhaps have never been written about before. These too have their own special beauty. Getting to know them you appreciate not only their own intrinsic value, in their unique positioning and their particular aspect and outlook, but also in their interlocking role in the greater background of whatever it was that was going on then in Iron Age North Wales.

Dinas, above Llanfairfechan, is modest by any standards, and with the great summit of Penmaenmawr fortified above it you cannot help wondering why it was necessary. The steep side is too sheer to need defences, and the double ramparts along the southern sides have almost disappeared. Actually the lines of defence can better be seen from a distance, and from the Roman road at Bwlch y Ddeufaen they are fairly clear. What Dinas has is what all hill-forts seem to have, a splendid view of wild Welsh country. From here you can see across to Anglesey, and perhaps to the nearest island fort at Din Sylwy; but that cannot have been Dinas' function, as it would perfectly well have been visible from the higher and larger fort on Penmaenmawr.

Above the Conwy valley, Caer Bach, at 1,300 feet on a slope of Tal y Fan, is what it claims to be, small in relation to most forts. It is a simple ringed hill, with the air of being nowhere special. The only striking thing about it is its line of sight to other hillforts. In an almost straight line you can see, looking north, Caer Lleon on Conwy Mountain and Pen Dinas on the Great Orme. Looking south you get a clear view of Pen y Gaer. As a relay point in a chain of signals Caer Bach makes a lot of sense.

Pen Dinas on the Great Orme shows, now, only very slight signs of its Iron Age use. From here you can see Bryn Euryn above Mochdre, where the fort of Dinarth was another of this close-knit group. The extensive hilltop there shows signs of banks on the east approach, but again nothing striking. Moving east along the coast Pen y Corddin above Llanddulas also has extensive views, but not, at least clearly, of any other hill-forts. It is a large well-defended compound, with abundant signs of workings within it, and room for the enclosure there of large flocks and herds, consistent with the good farming country all around.

Pen y Corddin was excavated in 1905 under the supervision of Dr Willoughby Gardner, revealing well-constructed masonry under the debris of fallen walls. The good preservation of the bottoms of these walls suggested that the tops had been deliberately thrown down. There were not a lot of useful finds (a solitary piece of pottery gave a likely date of occupation as the early centuries A.D.) and no permanent dwellings were identified. Refuse tips provide evidence of occupation, and sling stones suggest a garrison. The archeologist noted that the next fort in the coastal series, Castell Gwawr, 'is just visible across 1$^1/_2$ miles of high ground to the east'. This fact is not easily apparent today, since Castell Gwawr, now heavily afforested and itself inaccessible, forms part of a generally wooded scene in that direction.

Dr Gardner had more luck with his excavation at Dinorben, which is unusual in many respects. One of these is that it is no longer there. A vast hole gapes in the hillside which once bore it, evidence of an insatiable hunger for limestone.

It is unusual too in that we know a great deal about it. Most excavations of Iron Age forts have been disappointing. They have yielded little that can help us date their period, or periods, of occupancy, or tell us about the people who used them. Where they have been reticent, however, Dinorben has been prolific. From Dr Willoughby Gardner's excavations between 1912 and 1922, and the emergency excavations carried out by Dr H.N. Savoury in the 1950's and '60's, hundreds of objects, domestic, military and ornamental, have been found.

These are now in the National Museum of Wales in Cardiff. They reveal that Dinorben was in use as a place of settled habitation from as early as 300 B.C., though not then fortified. It was enclosed, but perhaps only to house stock, in the 2nd century B.C., and more substantially fortified in the early years of this era, presumably in response to the Roman advance. It occupancy ends about 150 A.D. when the walls were partly destroyed, evidently (as this happened elsewhere) as part of a general Roman policy. It was re-occupied in late Roman times, when coin-dating enables a confidence as to dates and indicates either a degree of Roman security or of neglectfulness, which permitted a native return to the hilltop citadel.

Dinorben, then, was occupied much more fully than appears to have been the case with many hillforts, and this leads us to view them, as a generalisation, as being of two types: those occupied by a garrison or temporary population, and those which were lived in by a large number of people over a long period. With its original open, undefended plan, and its gradual elaboration of increasingly strong defences, Dinorben testifies to four hundred years of growing conflict.

From the detailed excavations at Dinorben we can glean some facts about the way of life of the people who inhabited North Wales at the turn of the era. They lived at the edge of the old forest where red deer could be hunted, the horns of these making useful components in household objects. Having iron tools they were able to extend their forest clearings, as is evidenced by the large numbers of stock they raised, and during the period studied the emphasis shifted from sheep to cattle, the Early Iron Age people consuming an equal quantity of both but the people of the later Roman period slaughtering three times as many cattle as sheep, a figure consistent with the idea of increasing forest clearance.

There were signs of metal-working on the site, mainly of iron. In their later periods the people here used coins, as did all nations subject to Roman influence, and to a greater extent than many others they displayed the curious tendency to lose them which has been such a benefit to archeologists. They also lost a lot of pins and brooches, rather as we lose buttons, from which we know that they liked even small and functional objects to be elaborately decorated. Two fine ox-heads were evidently designed as parts of the handles of buckets, and relate these people's tastes not only to those of people in similar forts in many parts of Britain but also to those of their continental contemporaries. The ox-heads are interesting particularly as they represent a change in style from the abstract decorations of the traditional Celtic world to the naturalistic depictions favoured by Roman culture, though still, in this case, with very distinct Celtic stylisation. Our people, in other words, were becoming Romanised, at least by the second century A.D.

Dinorben seems to form the end of a string of hillforts on the north-west coast, but a further string runs right along the Clwydian hills inland, those border uplands between two highly prosperous areas, the Vale of Clwyd and the Cheshire plain. Foel Fenlli, the southernmost hill of the range, neighbouring the distinctive peak of Moel Famau, has one such hillfort on its summit. Steep-sided and round-topped, this high hill has much to recommend it as a fortifiable outlook. Its south-west slopes command an unparalleled view of the Vale of Clwyd, from end to end. Its 1,500 foot elevation might seem to give it little need for its double earthen bank defences. Nobody was ever going to storm Foel Fenlli. Nobody would arrive at its great embankments who wasn't out of breath.

The much easier modern path leaves from the car park at the top of the pass, and it is well worth the walk, if only to grasp the true outstandingness of Foel Fenlli's position. When you finally reach its breathtaking summit you see before you on the other side an equally astonishing view of the wide spread of the distant Cheshire plain.

After the end of their period of use as defended sites, the forts may in many cases have continued in occupation as farming compounds, with a lesser bank replacing the defensive wall which often seems to have been pulled down by the Romans. Whatever their subsequent use, it is clear that in their original form they were well fortified, from which we may draw a connection between them and troubled times. We long of course to know more. Who were these pre-Roman Welshmen defending themselves against, and why? Certainly the forts seem to be a response to a problem, rather than a mere convenience. They represent a significant amount of organised work, and imply by this a social system adequate for this organisation. Taking so many people off other work involves motivating them in some way to do so, since there is a cost involved.

In North Wales (as opposed to the Severn valley, on the Welsh border) most of the forts are within three miles of the sea. Even Pen y Gaer, over the Conwy valley, is close to the tidal river, and incidentally overlooks the route from that waterway to the nearby coast. The problem, then, might well be sea-borne, as it was in later times; it is supposed by some authorities that the evidence of successive periods of building indicates waves of invaders, the second occupants protecting themselves against a third, though of course this need not be so. The second style, where it occurs, a bank and ditch added to the original stone-built wall on the outside, may be simply a technical innovation.

There is in fact no reason to infer invaders at all, rather than, say, a continual pestilence of pirates or pillaging raiders, such as we know plagued the Aegean islands until almost modern times, causing the islanders to locate their settlements on the highest point of the island. In fact these hilltop citadels are reminiscent in siting of the villages there, except that in North Wales the largest quantity of hut remains is in many cases outside, rather than inside, the defending wall. There are notable exceptions, but in some cases at least the relatively few huts within the compound itself indicates use as a refuge rather than a permanent settlement. Garn Fadrun, for instance, on the Lleyn peninsula, has a number of large enclosures within the walls and a very small number of actual hut rings, but is surrounded by an extensive area of both. Pen y Gaer, in the Conwy valley, has few of both, with probably more undiscovered huts outside. It would be rash to generalise, however, since in other cases the forts were apparently constructed to house a whole nation. A hundred and seventy huts have been identified within the ramparts of Garn Boduan, also on the Lleyn, and a hundred and fifty lie within the walls of Tre'r Ceiri, nearby. One thing seems certain from the forts' positioning: they were not defending themselves against each other. There is no attempt to withdraw from one another; rather they are geographically linked, as in a chain.

The temptation to refer to a 'network' here might perhaps lead us to beg the question. It is striking though that from many of the hillforts you can see another hillfort, and from that in some cases a further one not visible from the first, so that a relay effect becomes a possibility. Thus from Pen Dinas on the Great Orme you can see the top of Bryn Euryn in the one direction, and looking in the other direction you can see Caer Lleon on Conwy Mountain, from where you can see to Caer Bach and Pen y Gaer; and also Allt Wen at the other end of the mountain, which in turn commands a free and expansive view of Braich y Dinas on Penmaenmawr, which in turn (along with Dinas above Llanfairfechan) looks in the north-west directly into Anglesey, where in the low-lying landscape prominences such as those providing the site of Din Sylwy, above Red Wharf Bay, and Caer y Tŵr on Holyhead Mountain, are visible over many miles.

In the Victorian age a series of semaphore stations was set up on a similar route, from Holyhead via the Great Orme and the uplands beyond Colwyn Bay, all the way to Liverpool. It was normal for a message to take less than five minutes to pass from Holyhead to Liverpool, and under test conditions it was shown that this could be done in twenty-three seconds. It is of course no proof that this was their purpose, but if the chain of hillforts in North Wales and western England did in fact (with the aid of occasional outposts) form a visual series, then it would have made sense for them to house garrisoned and defended beacons. Thus a column of smoke rising above Holyhead or at the foot of the Lleyn peninsula could send a message to Dinorben in a matter of minutes, greatly faster than a messenger could travel.

This would enable valuables such as cattle to be rounded up and taken into the defended compound, the walls manned, provisions stored, long before any pillagers arrived. This would have two notable results. It would enable a stable and secure economy to flourish in the catchment areas of the hillforts; and it would discourage the raiders from making that particular trip, knowing they would be returning empty-handed.

Whether or not the hillforts worked in that sort of way as a deterrent to casual raiders (and we must repeat that the fact that they could have done does not mean that they did), we know at least that they did not prove so effective against a more determined enemy. There is evidence that several of these forts ceased to be used, and that their walls were deliberately weakened, at about the time of the Roman invasion. We also know that the Romans did attack hillforts. Tacitus' description of Ostorius' assault on the stronghold of Caractacus is graphic, detailing as it does an instance of the use of the invulnerable defence known as the *testudo*, the linked roof of shields so called from its resemblance to a tortoise's shell, a weapon only effective of course against assault from above:

> On one side there were steep slopes. Wherever the gradient was gentler they piled stones into a kind of rampart . . . The defences were strongly manned . . . Ostorius led his eager soldiers forward. They easily crossed the river and came up to the rampart. But then, in an exchange of missiles, they came off worse in wounds and casualties. However, under a roof of locked shields, the Romans demolished the crude and clumsy stone embankment, and in the subsequent fight at close quarters the natives were driven to the hill-tops.

It may have been a reaction to the arrival of the Roman army that led to the apparent full-time occupation of secure sites such as Tre'r Ceiri, where excavation has proved that occupation continued well into the Roman period, and Garn Boduan, where Roman pottery has been found in a hut of evidently late construction; Braich y Dinas, also, which was excavated in 1912 before it was destroyed by quarrying, had a large number of huts within the ramparts and yielded finds dating to the period between the first and fourth century A.D., indicating that its main use was during the Roman period; whereas in the forts with few internal huts, such as Conwy Mountain and Pen y Gaer, no Roman period items have been found at all, indicating that these were attacked, cleared and destroyed by the arriving Romans. Comparing the quality of preservation of the walls of Tre'r Ceiri with others, such as for instance Conwy Mountain, one forms the impression that the more accessible forts were systematically ruined by the Romans to prevent their re-use, but that Tre'r Ceiri, at least, perhaps being outside the Romans's sphere of activity, perhaps simply too steep to tackle even with the *testudo*, survived, as did Braich y Dinas on the awesome summit of Penmaenmawr.

We may therefore envisage a situation in North Wales at around the time of Christ in which a settled and highly organised and numerous population had developed a system for carrying on their lives which overcame some persistent problem such as that of raiders. Confronted then with a radically new type of warfare they had to make a sudden and no doubt painful adaptation in defence of their precarious independence.

We move in the next chapter into this new world. History succeeds pre-history at this point, the point at which the artefacts of archeology, so hard to interpret with confidence, are supported as evidence by written records.

Bibliography

Archeology and Language. Colin Renfrew. Jonathan Cape.
The Celts. ed. Joseph Raftery. Mercier Press, Cork.
The Celts. T.G.E. Powell. Thames & Hudson.
The Coming of Iron. G.A. Wainwright. *Antiquity* March 1936, Vol. X No.37 p.5.
Tacitus on Britain and Germany. trs. H. Mattingly. Penguin.
Tacitus: The Annals of Imperial Rome. trs. Michael Grant. Penguin.
Caesar: The Conquest of Gaul. trs. S.A. Handford. Penguin.
The Druids. Nora K. Chadwick. University of Wales Press.
The Ancient Hill-Fortress on Pen-y-Gorddyn. Willoughby Gardner. Bedford Press.
Dinorben: A Hill-Fort Occupied in Early Iron Age and Roman Times.
Willoughby Gardner & H.N. Savoury. National Museum of Wales.
A Find of the Early Iron Age from Llyn Cerrig Bach, Anglesey. Sir Cyril Fox.

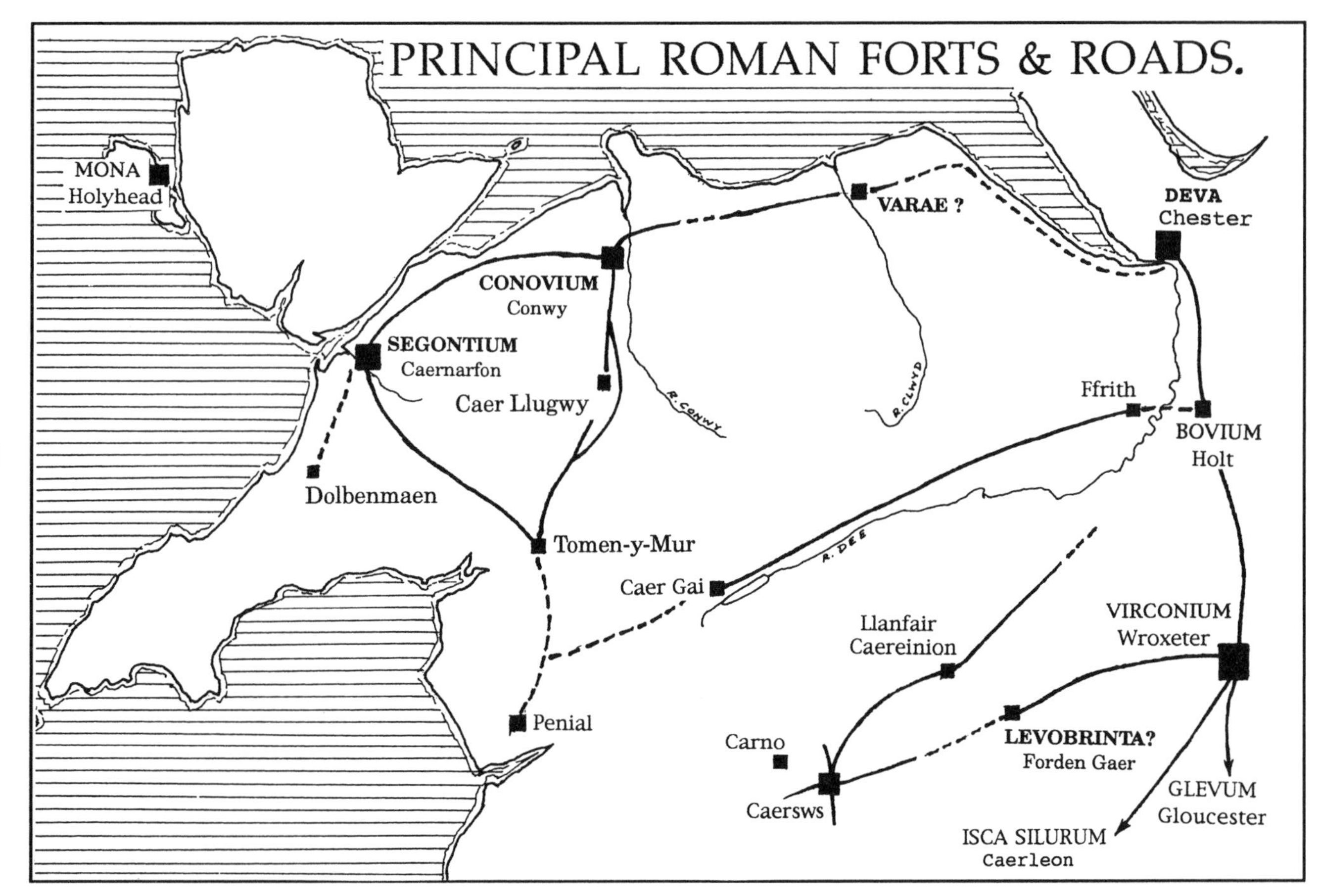
PRINCIPAL ROMAN FORTS & ROADS.
MONA
Holyhead
VARAE ?
DEVA
Chester
CONOVIUM
Conwy
SEGONTIUM
Caernarfon
Caer Llugwy
R. CONWY
R. CLWYD
Ffrith
BOVIUM
Holt
Dolbenmaen
Tomen-y-Mur
R. DEE
Caer Gai
Llanfair
Caereinion
VIRCONIUM
Wroxeter
Penial
Carno
LEVOBRINTA?
Forden Gaer
Caersws
GLEVUM
Gloucester
ISCA SILURUM
Caerleon

Outpost of Empire

Caesar gave his reasons for invading Britain in the first place, in his usual curt style:

> It was now nearing the end of summer, and winter starts early in those parts, since all that part of the coast of Gaul faces north. In spite of all this Caesar started to prepare for an expedition to Britain, **because he knew that in almost all the Gallic campaigns the Gauls had received reinforcement from the Britons.**

This is not generally seen as a compelling reason, and the challenge of subduing yet another country may have been as strong a motive. If Caesar knew that the Britons were backing up the Gauls, that was almost all he knew about them, and curiosity may have been a motive too. Certainly once there, he sets about describing the place in much detail.

His initial campaigns were focused on Kent, which seemed even by then to be the centre of social organisation. It may be supposed that it was from there that help had been sent to Gaul, since Caesar clearly says that the coastal areas were occupied by Belgic immigrants, the same people, that is, as he was fighting on the continent. There was a clear divide, in his perception, between these people and the population inland, 'people who claim, in their oral tradition, to be aboriginal'.

North Wales was a long way from the Romans' first areas of interest, and as a place and a people almost unknown to them. Caesar describes the west coast, which he mistakenly thinks faces Spain, and he even mentions what is clearly intended to be the Isle of Man – it lies midway between Britain and Ireland – though as he calls it 'Mon', later the Roman name for Anglesey, our first outside reference to North Wales is, ironically, accidental; our own valleys and mountains remained unknown to him, and his information then tails off into northern hazes with remarkable vagueness.

In any case these first tentative excursions into Britain left little mark, and they are only of interest as the prelude to the eventual campaigns which so radically affected our history. It is clear that the effort of getting to Britain, against the odds of bad weather in unknown seas (the Romans did not even know, until they set out, that Atlantic tides are higher at full moon) had not produced sufficient results, and in any case Caesar had considerable troubles in Gaul and elsewhere at this time which need not concern us, but no doubt influenced him. He did not come back to Britain.

In fact it was not until 43 A.D., in the reign of the emperor Claudius, that the invasion and occupation of Britain by Rome really started. Even then we in North Wales were a long way from the central events. Then and for a long time after that the concept of the province 'Britannia' was mainly confined to the south-east. The land was better there, minerals plentiful, the people probably more amenable to Roman 'pacification', and the terrain easier to control by the Roman military machine.

Outside the province of Britannia lay a different world, still very much the traditional world of the Celtic tribes. We know the names of several of their leaders, though (perhaps inevitably) in Latin form: we know of Cunobelinus, who became Shakespeare's Cymbeline; we know of the pro-Roman queen Cartimandua, ruler of the northern tribe of the Brigantes, and her husband Venutius, who eventually turned against her and led the resistance to Rome. We know of Boudicca, of course, or Boadicea, queen of the Iceni in the south. Prominent amongst all these great leaders, we know the name Caractacus.

It is true that we know of all of them, and of him, mainly from Tacitus, but it is also true that Tacitus seems to have been remarkably fair. He praises Rome's enemy Venutius as a great strategist. He does not seek to play down Cartimandua's cunning. It is through his vision that we see Caractacus as heroic.

It is by a series of chances that North Wales now first enters mainstream history. Caractacus, or as he is more correctly known, Caradoc, was not of the tribes of North Wales, the Ordovices, the Cornovii, the Deceangli or the Venedotae; he came from further south. His father was the great Cunobelinus, who ruled the territory between Norfolk and the Thames. When he himself inherited a kingdom it seems to have been in the neighbourhood of today's southern Home Counties, a long way, in other words, from the scene of his eventual fame.

At that time Wales was occupied largely by four tribes, though smaller groups slotted between them in the north. The Cornovii inhabited what is now the border area between Chester and Shrewsbury; the Ordovices were to the west and south of them, and further south again, (after a gap due probably to deficiency in the record rather than lack of population), lay the Demetae and the Silures. It was the last of these that Caradoc eventually joined, and in their territory that he started making trouble for Rome.

It seems that on the death of Cunobelinus another son, Togodumnus, succeeded as king of the territory lying to the north of the Thames. Of Caradoc's own early career we have only the meagre evidence of a coin found near Guildford, and a mention of his leading a force which the Romans defeated possibly at a site in Hampshire, under the first of the Governors of the new province, Aulus Plautius, at the very start of the intended pacification. It might have been as a result of that event that he joined the Silures.

Plautius was replaced as Governor in 47 A.D. by a man of considerable determination and ability, Ostorius Scapula. The situation had weakened considerably in the last years of his predecessor's rule, and the state of affairs Ostorius confronted was, Tacitus says plainly, chaotic. Taking advantage of the inexperience of a new commander and of the approach of winter, tribes which had not been brought within the Roman ambit began to invade the lands of the peaceful province. In this action we may see the start of Caradoc's campaign, and subsequent events identify the Silures, whom he now led, as one of the 'hostile tribes'.

Ostorius was not a man to panic; indeed his complete lack of nerves amounted to incaution, and eventually led him into an error of judgement. His first instinct was to move his light auxiliary at speed. He knew two things: that morale had to be restored at once, before a general decline set in; and that the campaigning season was almost over. The Roman army was too cumbersome a machine to fight effectively in the western hills in the winter. This quick action evidently caught the hostile tribes unprepared, and the opposition died down.

Tacitus' text is obscure at this point, but scholarly interpretation has produced a convincing picture of what happened next. To stop this sort of thing happening again, and hindering his task of stabilising the province, Ostorius decided to disarm the tribes along the border of Britannia.

The actual words can be translated 'on this side of the rivers Trent and Severn', indicating a border to the settled lands served by the Fosse Way, the great Roman highway running diagonally across England, between Lincoln and the West Country. This stipulation meant that there was no attempt to disarm the tribes of the west, the Silures and Ordovices and others who occupied the lands which are now Wales, so that for various reasons the decision itself seems to have been comparatively harmless. Firstly, the tribes within the disarmed area were supposed to be friendly to the Romans; secondly, they were theoretically supposed to have already been disarmed. The implication is that Ostorius did not trust them. Perhaps some of them had joined in the recent risings on the wrong side.

It is however with this act that the long and fierce campaign begins, which culminated in the defeat of Caradoc in North Wales. Faced with the removal of the weapons which they were not supposed to have, the supposedly friendly tribes started to rebel. They were at once supported by others, not even nominally friendly. First the Iceni in East Anglia, then, bringing the matter at last directly home to us, the Deceangli.

Tacitus actually writes 'Decangi', but archeology, in the form of some inscriptions on pieces of lead found in Flintshire, indicates that the tribe knew itself as the Deceangli. Their exact location is not certain, but with this slight evidence we may put them between the Venedotae and the Cornovii, and north of the Ordovices. It has been speculated that they may have been a sub-branch of the latter.

We know that in attacking them Ostorius 'nearly reached the sea facing Ireland'. The description of the campaign suits our territory. It was a scrappy little war of ambush and reprisal, in a land not made for pitched battle. Evidently however this north-west coastal tribe was rich. As he pressed coastwards into the deteriorating weather of a North Welsh autumn and towards unknown events Ostorius pillaged and robbed their land and took from them substantial booty.

Not for the last time North Wales was saved from permanent subjugation by a distraction taking place elsewhere. Ostorius was informed he had a more important enemy to quell than the distant Deceangli. The great northern nation of the Brigantes broke out in revolt, the buffer tribe which the Romans relied on between Britannia and the unknown and untamed wilds of the north of Britain, whose friendship was essential to the province's peace of mind.

The tribe of Deceangli cannot, in any case, have been one of his main concerns, and it is in fact hard to guess what prompted this expedition to the coast of North Wales. It could have been that Ostorius was anticipating a combination of the major tribes, and intended to set up a Roman presence in-between them. In view of what happened next it cannot have been the Deceangli themselves he was concerned with.

Having subdued the rebel element among the Brigantes, Ostorius turned his attention again to the Silures, and boldly invaded their territory. They were a temperamentally warlike people, and would not take this lightly. The result was a much larger-scale war than Ostorius had intended. It was, Tacitus tells us, Caractacus who inspired this rising: his 'many undefeated battles, and even many victories, had made him pre-eminent among British leaders'.

Of the many things we come to know in due course about Caradoc, what must strike us at this early stage is his remarkable ability to command allegiance over a wide stretch of Britain and among different tribal people. His campaign showed signs of reaching a national scale, and he presented the Romans with the one thing they feared and usually managed to avoid, a united enemy. He can only have done this by having at the same time a wide grasp of the political situation and a charismatic personality.

When Ostorius invaded the territory of the Silures, Caradoc was one move ahead of him. He mobilised the Ordovices, further north; in doing so he took the war into the fastness of North Wales. Here he established a base from which the enemies of Rome could operate in unison. 'Qui pacem nostram metuebant . . . ': 'all who feared Roman peace came to support him.'

This of course says a lot about Roman 'peace', if people feared it. It was needless to say a euphenism for subjugation. Tacitus says elsewhere, in his 'Agricola', that this fact was used in British resistance propaganda: 'Robbery, butchery, rapine,' says a rebel leader, 'the liars call Empire; where they have made devastation, they call it peace.'

Once again Ostorius did not hesitate. This alliance had to be broken, and if it meant confronting the enemy on terms which suited them, in the hill country of North Wales, he would do it. He gathered his forces and once again marched north.

Time has elapsed, evidently, unrecorded by Tacitus, in the campaign against the Silures and the mopping up of the Brigantean rebellion. It is now the eighth year of the war, presumably starting with the battles launched by Plautius on his arrival in 43 A.D. The date of the final battle is agreed as 51. Its precise location, we shall see, is more hotly disputed.

It was, it is clear, Caradoc who called the tune. He knew that it was impossible to avoid a battle, but also that he could choose its site. Tacitus tells us that he was inferior in strength of arms, in spite of the ploy of rallying all anti-Roman factions to his cause. To say, as he does then, that this was made up for by cunning and local knowledge is perhaps an understatement. It is obvious that Caradoc was a supreme strategist, and he had deliberately taken the war into an area which the Romans did not know at all.

It was, moreover, one which suited them badly. The Roman army worked effectively as a massed body, when its disciplined formation and substantial armours could present an impenetrable front and move with irresistable tank-like momentum. Ostorius had several times used his light auxiliary forces, which could move much faster and more flexibly that the main body of the legions. This, however, was to be no mere skirmish. This was not even a punitive expedition, as when Ostorius had before struck violently not at a tribe's existence but at their morale. There is no doubt that he had reached the point when the elimination of Caractacus was his sole aim, and for this the bulk of his army would be required.

The Romans would have preferred a pitched battle, but instead Caradoc presented them with a siege. It was, however a siege on one front only, since the site was chosen to give the Britons an escape route to the rear. This means that it must have been close to country which the Romans could not penetrate, which we must suppose to be high or precipitate ground. The fact that the native forces did not simply disappear into that territory at once, but awaited the approach of the Roman army, must be part of Caradoc's strategy. He was reconciled to a battle. He thought he could win it.

On one side there were steep hills. That left only one possible direction of approach. On that side, however, there was a river, and one which had no obvious crossing point. A stone rampart was built across the easier slopes, and this was heavily manned.

It is assumed from this that the river must have been a big one, and therefore it was very probably the Severn. Caer Caradoc, near Church Stretton, does not answer this description; nor does the other Caer Caradoc between Clun and Knighton, further south. These names of course commemorate the presence in this area of one of Britain's most heroic leaders, and the fact that he should be so closely associated with the area of the Severn valley encourages us to think of his stand against the Roman army being played out here. Caer Caradoc, north of Church Stretton and south of Wroxeter, is a particularly fine example of an Iron Age hillfort, such as the Romans would have encountered when they came, one of an apparent chain which runs southwards along the edge of the Shropshire and Cheshire plains, where, at the valleys of the Severn and the Dee, they meet the foothills of Wales. At 1,500 feet the peak of Caer Caradoc would have been a match for the Romans, even without its substantial ramparts. But such a site would of course have been too small for Caradoc to assemble his massed hordes, for this deciding battle on which he had staked his destiny.

He knew what it was that was at stake. He knew that with his own fate went that of his nation. He had undoubtedly a sense of history, and saw that this was one of its turning points. Indeed so vehement was his determination and the enthusiasm with which he inspired his people that a tremor of it reached the Roman camp. Down in the valley they heard the cheers rising over the stone ramparts on the slope above them as Caradoc made his speech. It must have been for them a frightening roar. They knew, or imagined, the words which had aroused it, and Tacitus reports them as if he had been there.

This is the day, and this is the battle, he said, which will either free us as a nation or else enslave us for ever. It is no less than that. We have been in this situation before. Your ancestors confronted the mighty Julius Caesar, and showed him of what stuff they were made. By standing up to him then they preserved their people, we, that is, who stand here now, from Roman domination. By their determination then they kept the blood of our nation free of foreign impurity. Now it is our task to carry on their struggle.

Every man swore by his own tribal oath that he would not accept defeat, no matter what weapons were brought against him nor what wounds resulted.

The Romans were already made uneasy by the river, before they even heard the cheering. Evidently it was in flood. Evidently also the native fortifications were close above it on the other side, so that it acted as a castle moat: emerging from the water you at once had to withstand the rain of sling-stones. The presence of the defenders was also only too apparent. Tacitus does not say so, but from other accounts we may imagine them as being frighteningly war-painted with woad.

The Romans resorted to their spirit of comradeship, the carefully nurtured team-spirit which kept them always acting as a body and supported their morale. They egged each other on. Their officers tapped this current and encouraged it. The matter would be conducted in the end with all the confidence of an invincible force.

Reconnaissance parties had identified the points of weakness among the unpleasant overhanging cliffs above them. The river did not prove the problem which its foaming surface had made them fear. They found a fording point. With Ostorius leading them, they crossed.

Once under the ramparts they were at a clear disadvantage.

The defenders above rained down on them rocks and sling-stones, and although the Romans responded with missiles from below they had gravity against them, so that initially they came off worse in wounds and injuries. It was then that they resorted to the testudo.

So effective a strategy is this that one wonders why they had not approached in this way from the start. As we mentioned in the previous chapter, this roof of shields proved to be the vanquisher of the strength of the hillforts. Locked together over the legionaries' heads they provided an impenetrable shell, under which they could march relentlessly forward. They reached and pulled down the ramparts, and were on the hilltop then fighting hand to hand.

The natives were driven back, and took their escape route into the hills, with the Romans after them. Ostorius' policy was to destroy them, this time, not just defeat them. His more mobile auxiliaries pursued them up the slopes with javelins, while the bulk of the army came after in their close-packed files. The British had no armour. If they fought back against the auxiliaries they risked having to withstand the swords and spears of the regular forces following them. They had no opportunity to stand and fight, pressed by either the light or the heavy army.

'It was a great victory.' Suddenly we remember which side Tacitus is on. If he were not so even-handed in his reporting it would be a great disadvantage to historians to have only the one viewpoint. Quite soon in our telling of North Wales' story we shall be able to listen to the voices of our own people. Up to this point it is temporarily true that history is told by the winning side. The druids could write, but they chose not to. It is not until the coming of Christianity that monks and priests (freed of the old Druidic superstition) started to write things down.

Tacitus' fairness in the meantime is compelling. You really feel he cared about Caractacus, as he tells the next part of the story. His wife and daughter were captured, his brothers surrendered, but he himself escaped.

It was at this point that he made a rare mistake, which was fatal both for himself and for the future of independent Britain. He fled to Cartimandua, queen of the Brigantes. How could he not know that just as he had staked his destiny on resisting the Romans, so she, with rather more realism, had staked hers on appeasing them? How could he not know that she had split the Brigantes on this very issue, and by cunning and determination got her way? Did he not know, as we do, that Cartimandua was a ruthless politician?

His wife and daughter, and his brothers, were of course already in Rome, when he arrived, in chains but still a hero, surrounded by the glory of his fame. The people of Rome flocked to see the man who had stood up to their empire's might, and the Emperor Claudius spotted a chance to glorify himself. He turned the event into a public spectacle, in which he and Caractacus were to be the star performers. The people were called to the public square, where a guard-of-honour stood before the barracks. The procession of the victory came through the streets. First the lesser prisoners, the minor chiefs who had rallied to Caractacus. Then the spoils of war, the emblems and symbols of defeated powers. Then the leader's family. Then the man himself.

Although the other prisoners were intimidated by the situation and the display of power, and demeaned themselves before the emperor,

Caractacus showed no signs of fear. Perhaps anticipating a robust reaction Claudius had provided him with a podium, and he spoke.

> If my lineage and my rank had been supported with a degree of success, I should have come to this city as friend and not as prisoner, and you would not have been too proud to ally yourself with one of such noble birth and who is the ruler of so many nations. As things are, mine is the humiliation, yours the glory. Once I had horses, men, arms and wealth. Are you surprised that I am sad to lose them? Because you want to rule the world, does it follow that others must welcome enslavement?

As it is, he said, Claudius' fame was his hostage; it depended on his own.

> If I had surrendered without a blow before being brought before you, neither my defeat nor your victory would have become famous. If you execute me now, they will both be forgotten. Let me live, and I shall be a permanent symbol of your mercy.

It was, of course, a cunning speech, and it succeeded. Claudius could see the sense of the proposal. He pardoned and freed the chieftain and his family.

Meanwhile back in Britain, deprived of his chief enemy, Ostorius lost much of his impetus. The effects on North Wales of the defeat of Caradoc take the form of a stabilising of the border. It was probably as a result of the policy which Ostorius formed then that the great Roman fort of Viroconium, now Wroxeter, was constructed, under the shadow of the native hillfort on the Wrekin and within sight of that on Caer Caradoc. From pottery finds it is known that the first fort at Viroconium was occupied then, and we also know that it became at once the base of the 20th Legion, one of the forces which Ostorius brought north to combat Caractacus. It seems therefore that the Romans did not simply defeat the British leader and go back to their settled province. Their presence on the border of North Wales was established by that event. On the other hand they did not then press further north to Chester or west into North Wales, as we might have expected such a victorious force to do. As a result of this, as well, North Wales retained sufficient independence to fight again.

In fact the Romans rather turned their attention to the south, and Ostorius resumed his bitter struggle with the Silures, which eventually wore him out. He died *'taedio curarum fessus'*, – 'exhausted by the strain of cares'. It was not until three governors later that the Romans paid heed to North Wales again.

When they did, it was to be the start of a pattern which has radically affected the way our area has developed. That is, it set the structure of advance from a base at Chester via a linked series of forts to the western coast, the form which has been followed by so many invaders and lines of communication that it has ultimately determined the layout of our land. That it happened in the first place was, however, due to the combination of background factors with personal qualities.

Caesar came to Britain, he says, because it was assisting the Gauls in their resistance. It was for the same reason that Suetonius came to Anglesey. We have seen in the last chapter that the Druid religion appears to have been based there, and perhaps it was that that enabled Anglesey to be a threat to Roman peace by 'feeding the native resistance'. It is also the case, of course, that Anglesey could have been feeding the rebels in a more literal sense, and certainly, as we shall see, it was always a good military strategy to attack and burn Anglesey at harvest time.

There had been a quick succession of governors after Ostorius. Didius, his successor, was old for the job, and governed by delegation; he was chosen because of his experience and the respect gained from a distinguished career. Veranius, who governed next, died within a year of his arrival, and no advance took place. Then, crucially for North Wales, came Suetonius Paulinus.

Suetonius was an experienced and distinguished soldier. More significantly, his experience was in mountain warfare. In North Africa, he had crossed the Atlas mountains, the first Roman to do so. The uplands of Britain had no terrors for him.

Suetonius at once set about proving his reputation. He was an ambitious man. He had set his aim as outdoing all his rivals in popular reputation, and had finally to prove himself against a contemporary with whose career he had been competing for some time, a man called Corbulo, who at the time had overtaken him in popular adulation by the reconquest of Armenia.

It is on such slight things that history hangs. No doubt it is true that Anglesey was feeding the national resistance. As a reason for attacking it that is adequate. As a motive, though, how much more powerful is the desire to get one up on Corbulo.

We have already mentioned, in considering Druidism in the last chapter, Tacitus' reference to the part played by the druids in the defence of Anglesey. There is no doubt from his description that superstitious fear for a time affected the Roman legions.

Suetonius had planned the attack with care. We do not know for certain that the legionary fortress of Chester was already in existence, but assume that he based his invasion there, since it would enable him to supply his army by sea as it progressed and have ships at hand for the crossing of the Menai Strait. We know that on the occasion of the second invasion sixteen years later the inhabitants of Anglesey were expecting the army to be supported by a fleet, and since this is a surprising detail it must be due to their previous experience. Tacitus tells us that flat-bottomed boats were built for the crossing, and although of course they could have been built on the Caernarfon bank this was in enemy territory. If a Roman fort existed at Chester at that date the boats were built on the Dee and ferried round the coast. We do not know this, however; we have no firm date for Chester before 79 A.D., when a stamp on a lead water pipe gives us that as the start of the city's permanent occupation, in the time of the governorship of Agricola.

At any rate the building of the flat-bottomed boats indicates some local knowledge, since we are told that they were needed to deal with the shifting shallows, so that evidently Suetonius had had the area reconnoitred before he approached. The infantry crossed in the boats. He had with him two complete legions, amounting to some six thousand men, as well as four thousand mercenaries and auxiliaries. In addition to this formidable force he brought a troop of cavalry. Evidently they crossed on a broad front, since some of the horses were able to use fords, while others swam, their riders swimming beside them. The mention of shallow water means that the tide was out.

It was not until they had started to cross that they saw what awaited them. The shore of the Anglesey bank was thick with defenders; they lined it in a dense armed mass. This, to the Romans, was of course a familiar sight; it was an enemy force, and such as they were trained to deal with. What they were not prepared for was the sight of the women.

They are described as being like black furies, and it was the fact that they were other-worldly in appearance that frightened the troops. No doubt they were shrieking. They certainly carried flaming torches, as they ran in and out of the troops in a sort of ritual dance. The wild-haired women were one feature which made the scene look more than military. The other factor was the presence of the druids.

Standing still with their hands raised to heaven, the priesthood stopped the Romans in their tracks with the howl of what they knew to be terrible curses. They stood for a moment absurdly vulnerable between the boats and the battle-line, on the Anglesey beach:

> . . . our soldiers being so scared by the unfamiliar sight that their limbs were paralysed, and they stood motionless and exposed to be wounded.

They shook themselves out of this coma (as their general, with desperate urgency, exhorted them) by chiding each other for fearing a bunch of mad women. The standard bearers moved up the beach, and the troops mechanically followed. The druids had relied on their gods to save them, but the gods had finally let them down. There on the Anglesey shore they had abdicated, clearing the way for the eventual arrival of the new religion. That moment was effectively the end of the rule of the old one in Britain.

The druids were cut down where they stood, as if they had been trees. The wild women's torches were turned on themselves, and flames, enveloping the ground around, engulfed them. The Roman troops moved fast to garrison the island, making it Roman territory. One of the first things which Suetonius ordered them to do was to destroy the sacred groves. We know from our continental sources that the druids worshipped in oak groves – indeed, that is how they got their name, from 'derw', meaning 'oak'. Tacitus briefly justifies this act of sacrilege, and probably reflects current Roman propaganda: the druid religion was devoted to cruel superstition and they practised human sacrifice. Indeed it was their duty to cover their altars with the blood of captives, and to consult their gods through the use of human entrails. For a moment we inevitably recall the slave-chains which formed such a notable element among the finds at Llyn Cerrig Bach, and a cult of human sacrifice is of course quite possible; but much of what we know of Druidism shows it to have been concerned mainly with teaching and philosophy.

It is by one of those chances that govern history and stops it going as planned by human will that Anglesey did not at that time become a full colony of the Roman world. Perhaps it would have been a less independent place in subsequent times (and today) if it had done. No sooner had Suetonius done his destructive work than he had to leave.

He had, as Tacitus puts it in 'Agricola', 'exposed himself to a stab in the back'. The Iceni in Norfolk had risen in revolt under Boudicca, and had been joined by other tribes. While Suetonius was in Anglesey the province had almost been lost. The forced march south, the loss of London and St Albans, the final confrontation with Boudicca's hordes and the relief of hard-won victory are part of the grand drama of British history, but cannot, unfortunately, concern us here. Here we may wonder in what state his violent invasion and his sudden departure left North Wales.

The druid religion had been dealt a blow to the heart. Although it was probably not entirely destructible it could never be so centrally organised again. When Christianity eventually reached the province the remnants of the old religion were submerged, for the rest of Roman rule and during the post-Roman conflicts, and only emerged again in the early Middle Ages in the form of tales.

On the ground, the effect of the invasion mainly took the form of the route of a road, no doubt with temporary campaign-camps at the spots, the tactically crucial fording points of rivers, which were to be the sites of future Roman forts. Thus we have, originating from Suetonius' campaign, the basic structure of our modern settlement pattern, based on the linking of a chain of key points to Chester.

All this infrastructure was to come into use again, and take a more recognisable permanent form, some sixteen years later. In between the inhabitants of North Wales were clearly not defeated, or even cowed. The Roman presence on the borders of North Wales was based at the time at Wroxeter, where the fort of Viroconium had been in existence since the 50's, following the fall of Caractacus. Here it was that the 20th Legion had its base, and probably at this time the outpost fort at Chester was beginning to be used.

In the late summer of 77 A.D. an event took place which shook the Roman colony and might have marked a revival in national resistance similar to the blow dealt by Boudicca, had the personality of the man most directly concerned been at all different.

A troop of Roman cavalry found themselves stationed in hostile territory, an unpleasant, and, as it turned out, lethal situation. The tribe of the Ordovices, in whose lands they were, ambushed them one day while they were out on an exercise, and almost destroyed the whole squadron. This event is supposed to have taken place in the defile under Bryn Euryn, where the road now runs from Colwyn Bay to Mochdre, through which one would pass if coming along the coast from Chester and making for the Conwy valley.

This location for this critical event however has a number of flaws. What would the Ordovices be doing so far north and west – unless of course they controlled the territory of the Deceangli at this time? But Tacitus would then have attributed the deed to the Deceangli. What would a troop of cavalry be doing so far from Viroconium? It would be a rash general who would station important troops so deep into uncontrolled territory and so far from possible support. Why would they be coming along the coast, from where and to where would they be going, if this site is right? Even if they were an outpost of the infant fort at Chester (and we have no evidence that that was in existence until two years later) and making for the field-camp left by Suetonius at Canovium in the Conwy valley (and it is mere speculation that any fort was there until at least the following year) they would have been more sensible to use the Roman road which came down to the valley directly by an inland route. It makes no sense to see either the victims or the ambushers near Colwyn Bay.

The event, wherever it took place, had immediate results. It dealt a blow to the morale of the Roman army, at the time recently recovered from a period of uncertainty following the Boudiccan revolt. The feared loss of the province had precariously been overcome, and put into reverse. It was not a good time for this revival of confidence to be upset.

When Agricola took over as Governor of Britain the summer was already half over, and though this critical event had just taken place it was considered by both the Roman troops and their enemies to be too late in the year for the major campaign which would be expected in response. As a result the legions were dispersed in their home camps and the auxiliaries were all over the country. Agricola began to assert himself at once. He called the forces together, and set out for the hills.

Characteristically the Ordovices would not risk a pitched battle, much to the Romans' discomposure. Instead of waiting for them in a siege strategy, as Ostorius did with Caractacus, Agricola instead marched straight into the mountains of North Wales. It was, to put it mildly, a bold move. Some might say rash. But it paid off.

Perhaps because the Ordovices were not expecting this their defences were inadequate. The Romans had by now some experience of assaulting their hillforts. It is at this period that many of those fell out of use, their well-built ramparts slighted into the apparently haphazard pile of stones they now appear. When dealing with Agricola as a person Tacitus departs from his usual impartiality. Agricola was his father-in-law. Tacitus married his daughter in the very year that Agricola subdued North Wales.

Having marched into the mountains in the lead of his troops, 'to lend his own courage to the rest by sharing their peril', he then 'cut to pieces almost the whole fighting force of the nation' of the Ordovices, at least according to his son-in-law. We must doubt the totality of this massacre. We know how easily the Ordovices could evaporate into the hills; when Ostorius thought he had massacred them before, they were still very much there, and it seems certain that enough of them escaped Agricola to form a continuing threat.

Having attacked in the mountains he did not stop there. He knew no doubt, since he would not take up his governorship without studying its history, that Suetonius had considered it important to control Anglesey, but had been thwarted by circumstances from realising this ambition. Agricola decided to consolidate his gains. It is from this decision that the permanent occupation of North Wales by Rome begins.

This, it turns out, was a hurried decision, taken on the spot after the first victory. There was no supportive fleet, no flotilla of flat-bottomed boats. Yet its very spontaneity worked for its success. The inhabitants of Anglesey, still very much there, in spite of Suetonius' efforts, knew, of course, that they would be visited again. They did not know when, but looked for signs of preparation on the Roman side.

Agricola picked his lighter troops, the auxiliaries, and those among them who could swim. He then sent them across largely without arms. By bringing to bear the full force of surprise he was in fact adopting his enemy's tactics. It was a guerrilla attack. It proved remarkably effective.

Waiting for the fleet to come they were unprepared for this assault, and the result in Anglesey was panic and disorder. The island surrendered to Agricola at once, and he found himself enjoying sudden fame.

The first fort at Caernarfon, or Segontium, of which we have any trace started to be built about 100 A.D., so that if Agricola used that site as a base for his assault on Anglesey his wooden campaign-camp has disappeared. The extension of it in the 120's under Hadrian indicates a policy of controlling North Wales by a strong presence in its most western part. Anglesey itself however remained for a long time uncolonised; it seems to have been sufficient to control it from Segontium. As we shall see shortly, the Roman works on Anglesey are of later date.

That Canovium in the Conwy valley also started to be built in stone soon after 100 shows that the two formed part of a single strategy, and we know that they were linked by a road. The route from Chester to Caernarfon in fact forms the backbone of the Roman presence in North Wales.

Chester itself became a legionary headquarters early. The Second Auxiliary Legion was posted there from their first base in Lincoln some time in the 70's A.D. It grew during the next decade to become the largest fort in Roman Britain and to become the home of the eminent 20th Legion, which was moved there from their first base at Viroconium in the early 90's. Chester was the better focal point from which to carry on the northern campaigns.

It lay between the two major tribes, the Ordovices and the Brigantes; it could be supplied by sea up the river Dee, which could also be crossed at this point; and it gave an easy route into the newly conquered territory of North Wales.

In addition to Segontium and Canovium, there was a lesser fort on the Clwyd near St Asaph, called Varae, some artefacts from which are in the Grosvenor Museum in Chester.

The road between these places was an important element of the Roman plan. It enabled a network of support to maintain the series of forts in some security in enemy country It enabled great speed of movement over great distances, which gave to the Roman empire one of its most powerful weapons, an information system which could keep news and instructions flowing between a centralised command structure and its most remote outposts. Both mail and personnel could travel the empire at the rate of up to two hundred miles in twenty-four hours, by a system of 'mansiones', in effect posting points, which set the form later used by our own coach route system of post-houses or coaching inns, where horses could be exchanged and people victualled. We can still see the great Roman roads in North Wales today, where they run across upland moorland. In many other places they have disappeared under cultivation or under the lanes and tracks of subsequent times.

The Antonine Itinerary was a road-book made almost as soon as the roads were completed, in the 2nd century A.D., revised to the form in which we have it in the 3rd. It names this highway Iter XI, route 11. Enough of the route has been discovered and excavated for us to know how it was made. The technique varied according to the terrain. Near Chester, where the soil was soft and the road no doubt much used, it lay on a foundation of sandstone blocks. In the harder soil of the uplands it was formed of a number of small flat stones hammered to form a smooth surface. Although its exact route it lost for certain stretches above the Conwy valley its route through the hills to the west is clear enough.

At Caerhun in the valley itself lay one of the main forts, as we have mentioned, Canovium, the Latinisation of the old Celtic name Conwy. It formed a protection of the important river crossing set strategically on its further bank. Not much of Canovium can be seen now at Caerhun, only some mounds and banks in the fields beside the river and the occasional lumps of masonry from its walls which show the use of imported Cheshire sandstone, and remind us that this fort too was placed so as to be capable of supply by sea. It fell out of use in about 180 A.D., but its main period of occupation was in the early years of the second century, when it was occupied by the 19th Legion.

It is sometimes speculated that the Roman presence at Canovium had other motives in addition to the protection of the river crossing. They were known to be impressed by the quality of British pearls, and the fresh-water-mussel pearls of the Conwy river have for many centuries been famous. There was a supply of copper on the Great Orme which there is evidence the Romans knew of and used. In the valley itself there were other minerals, though no evidence of their Roman use, and the chalybeate spa waters of Trefriw would have been of great interest to them had they known of them, keen water-therapists that they were; but there is unfortunately no reason for us to think that they did. Though there are many reasons why the Romans might have had a special interest in the Conwy valley, we can only be certain of the military importance of the river crossing.

At the start of the 120's this, along with many other Roman forts, had their manpower considerably depleted by the massive effort of constructing Hadrian's Wall. Evidently North Wales was relatively safe by then, whereas the main problem now lay in the north. If a permanent fort at once replaced the field fort which we may presume Agricola built on the Conwy, then the Romans had been in the Conwy valley for over a hundred years by the time they started to withdraw. Later Roman coins found in the excavations at Caerhun indicate that a garrison remained here until 410 A.D., but since the Roman army had effectively left by then we may suppose the fort to have been used by Romanised Britons in the years following the Roman withdrawal. Finds of later coins in this area also indicate that there continued to be movement to and from the Great Orme, the copper of which remained in great demand for the minting of those same coins.

Coins and pottery have also provided a precise dating structure for Segontium, the regional centre which eventually became Caernarfon. The fort which Agricola originally founded after his assault on Anglesey was again replaced in stone on the same site. Sandstone from Cheshire and tiles from the Roman factory at Holt were imported here too, and although finds are scarce during the period of the building of Hadrian's Wall, from 120 to 140, here, unlike Canovium, the Roman presence increased considerably after 140. There were of course valuable sources of copper on Anglesey as well, which had to be protected, and this furthest west of the Romans major forts in Wales formed an important link in their encircling network which surrounded the mountainous heartland.

The Roman works on Anglesey, as has been mentioned, are of a later date than those on the mainland. The fort at Holyhead, a wall of which is prominently visible near the church, dates from the 3rd to 4th century, a time when other Roman forts were being vacated. It testifies to a lingering need to protect the island from invasion, and no doubt the copper mines on Parys Mountain across the top of the island were still of value, in the aftermath of the empire. More remarkable is a complete village of apparently mixed dates which was surrounded with a defensive wall in the 4th century. This, Din Lligwy near Moelfre on the eastern side of the island, has a number of round huts in the native tradition, and also some square ones, the rectilinear form of which testifies to Roman influence. The well-built and well-planned air of the whole village also suggests Roman thoroughness and attention to detail, so that probably what we have here is a villa-complex, the Romanised Britons' equivalent of a native tribal homestead. It indicates a degree of stability here in Anglesey which we would not expect at this transitional time.

South from Segontium and south from Canovium ran two more roads, which connected at Tomen y Mur above Trawsfynydd and then ran southwards together to South Wales, all the way in fact to the major Roman centre of Maridunum, now Carmarthen. On their separate links both roads had minor forts to act as posting points, some ten to twelve miles out on their journey. These are little visible now and lay long neglected, their existence a matter of speculation. Antiquarians had recorded remains of Roman buildings on a bend of the river Llugwy below Capel Curig, but these had disappeared by this century and it was not until the early 1920's that the site was investigated. Its dates of occupation were identified as between 90 and 140 A.D., and its shape as that of the familiar Roman rectangle.

The site of Caer Llugwy lies between the old coach road and the river, where the fast-flowing Llugwy does a spectacular right-angle bend, followed by a broad loop around the site of the fort. There are signs of raised banks, and in a clump of trees in the middle of the field are clear remains of a series of buildings. The strong flow of the deep, brown, silky river, on the very bank of which the small fort was sited, gives the place its main atmosphere today. At the other posting-point at Dolbenmaen, between Segontium and Tomen y Mur, there is even less to see.

Up at Tomen y Mur itself, where the roads meet and start their long journey south, the prevailing atmosphere is one of exposure to wild upland weather.

The visible remains at Tomen y Mur now consist of some fragments of Roman wall and a large mound which is not Roman but probably a medieval motte. Nearby are the remains of Roman baths, an area which is thought to have been an amphitheatre. It is an unusual site for a Roman camp, a hilltop setting looking across the lake to the Rhinog mountains and backed by high extensive moorland. Roman camps usually occur on flat level ground and low-lying sites. There is much that is remarkable about Tomen y Mur, not least its association with events in Welsh mythology, though these are often linked to Roman sites.

The road which ran southward from Canovium via the fort at Llugwy and joined the Segontium road here is still known, as it always was, as Sarn Helen, Helen's causeway. This name too connects the Roman works in this area with myth, supposedly being called after Elen, the local princess who married the hero of the Mabinogion story, 'The Dream of Macsen Wledig'. The use of the name however may be connected with another 'Elen', Helena, the Christian mother of Constantine the Great. It was during the time of her husband Constantius and their son Constantine that the full network of roads in Britain became established. There is an alternative and less romantic theory that the 'Helen' name of this and other roads is a corruption of 'Y Leng', meaning 'of the legions'.

Whatever the origin of its name our North Wales stretches of Sarn Helen run straight and clear across the moorland, often easily identifiable and visible (for instance where it runs north-east from Pont-y-pant in the Lledr valley), although in many other places its route is lost or debatable.

Just as the name of Elen may link us to history by way of Helena, so the story of her marriage to Macsen also refers to clear historical events. Segontium, like many other Roman forts, appears to have been abandoned in 383 A.D. Its coming into being and its evacuation then are described in mythology in the form of a simple and lovely tale.

The Emperor Macsen came to Caernarfon and married the lady Elen, because he had fallen in love with her in a dream. Following the dream's details his messengers had discovered her in her castle at the mouth of the river Seiont. All went well for a time, but his prolonged absence led to a rival emperor being appointed to his throne in Rome. Macsen in due course took all the troops he could muster from Britain and marched to attack his rival.

The story is based on that of the British-appointed usurper Magnus Maximus, and the depletion of the Roman garrisons in 383 is due to his mustering of troops to fight the rightful Emperor in Gaul, in 383. This was the beginning of the end of Roman rule in Britain, and it is interesting that the story should relate its origin so precisely to North Wales. There are hints that Magnus Maximus was at least not unknown here, but none that he was directly connected with Caernarfon. A coin bearing his image has been found there, showing his reign to have been sufficiently well established to have coinage minted and for it to have found its way so far west. Coins of the Empress Helena, the mother of Constantine and by confusion the princess Elen, wife of Macsen, have also been found at Segontium. More interestingly, indicating perhaps a closer association, the parish church just outside the Roman fort is dedicated to St Peblig, the Welsh adaptation of Publicius, who was the son of Magnus Maximus.

The Roman withdrawal from Britain was not caused by this single event, but rather by the proliferation of troubles on all the empire's borders. Britain was in effect abandoned as expendable. There were greater priorities. But though the troops left, the influence of the empire was more durable, and the Roman forms and customs underlay the development of British history and to some extent remain with us still.

In North Wales the effects of these are mainly discernible in the land-use and the settlement pattern which developed. Every large Roman camp or town was surrounded by a cultivated area, the 'prata'. We have to remember that a town like Chester was the home to several thousand people, as well as a large number of horses. This meant that the cultivation of the Cheshire plain, and the Shropshire plain around Viroconium, started early. Areas of the Conwy Valley and the hinterland of Caernarfon were also cleared and farmed at this time. This made such areas valuable, and tempting to invaders. We may see that when the Anglo-Saxons eventually came to the Cheshire plain they distinguished between the cultivated and the wooded areas in their use of place-names.

Those ending in 'ton' were already cleared; those in 'ley' were still then woodland. To a large extent the after-effects of Roman work determined the bases and the spread of the subsequent kingdoms.

More generally the Roman villa system, in which a large house would be supported by a farmstead, eventually gave rise in Britain as a whole and hence in North Wales to the system of country houses, which took the form of the manor house with its accompanying home farm. In many fully settled Roman countries the concept of central government gave rise to a new and permanent political order; but not in North Wales. Roman rule here was never complete enough to eradicate our native tribalism, and although the concept of the centrally governed nation was experimented with in post-Roman times by the setting up of 'High Kings', the unit of politics remained the small kingdom, in effect an extended tribe.

Bibliography

Roman Britain. (Oxford History of England). Peter Salway. Oxford.
Rome against Caratacus. Graham Webster. Batsford.
Works of Caesar and Tacitus, as previous chapter.
Sarn Helen, John Cantrel and Arthur Rylance, Cicerone.
Caernarfon – Segontium. National Museum of Wales.
Segontium and the Roman Occupation of Wales. R. Mortimer Wheeler. Honourable Society of Cymmrodorion.

The Post-Roman Decline

'After that,' states Gildas plainly, 'Britain was plundered of all her armed soldiery, her military forces . . . and, entirely ignorant of the ways of war, she was stunned and groaning for many years under the feet of two fiercely savage nations from across the seas, of the Scots from the north-west and the Picts from the north.'

From across the seas? Gildas implies a non-British source for these onslaughts, and indeed we might see the Scots mentioned here as being the people of Ireland, who had started to colonise Scotland shortly after the Roman departure. *'Scotti'* in Latin is used to indicate the same people as *'Hibernii'*. These people formed kingdoms in southern Wales, that of Demetia, modern Dyfed, and in southern Scotland of Dal Riada in Argyll. The Irish may therefore be seen as these overseas Scots.

The Picts however were clearly not an overseas nation, since they occupied the rest of Scotland. Gildas might be using the word *'transmarinis'* to mean simply 'foreign', but he had other words available to him to mean that. From the point of view of our present interests it is tempting to see *'trasmarinis'* as implying that these enemies all came by sea.

Gildas was writing in the second half of the sixth century of a time two hundred years before, but his is the earliest voice we have. He was a cleric of northern origin who was probably based at the time in Brittany. His information is supported by another, slightly later, source, this time directly from North Wales.

Nennius was also a cleric and was based in Bangor. About the year 800 he wrote down all the historical and legendary material he could find. He was conscious of the deficiency of his sources, 'since the scholars of the island of Britain had no knowledge, and put no records in books'. He had, he said, 'made a heap of all that I have found', and he supports his complaint by saying that he worked from the records of the Romans, the church, the Irish and even the English, as well as from oral tradition. This confirms what we have already observed, the long-held habit in Wales of refusing to write things down.

Nennius confirms Gildas' tale of overseas invasions by the Irish,

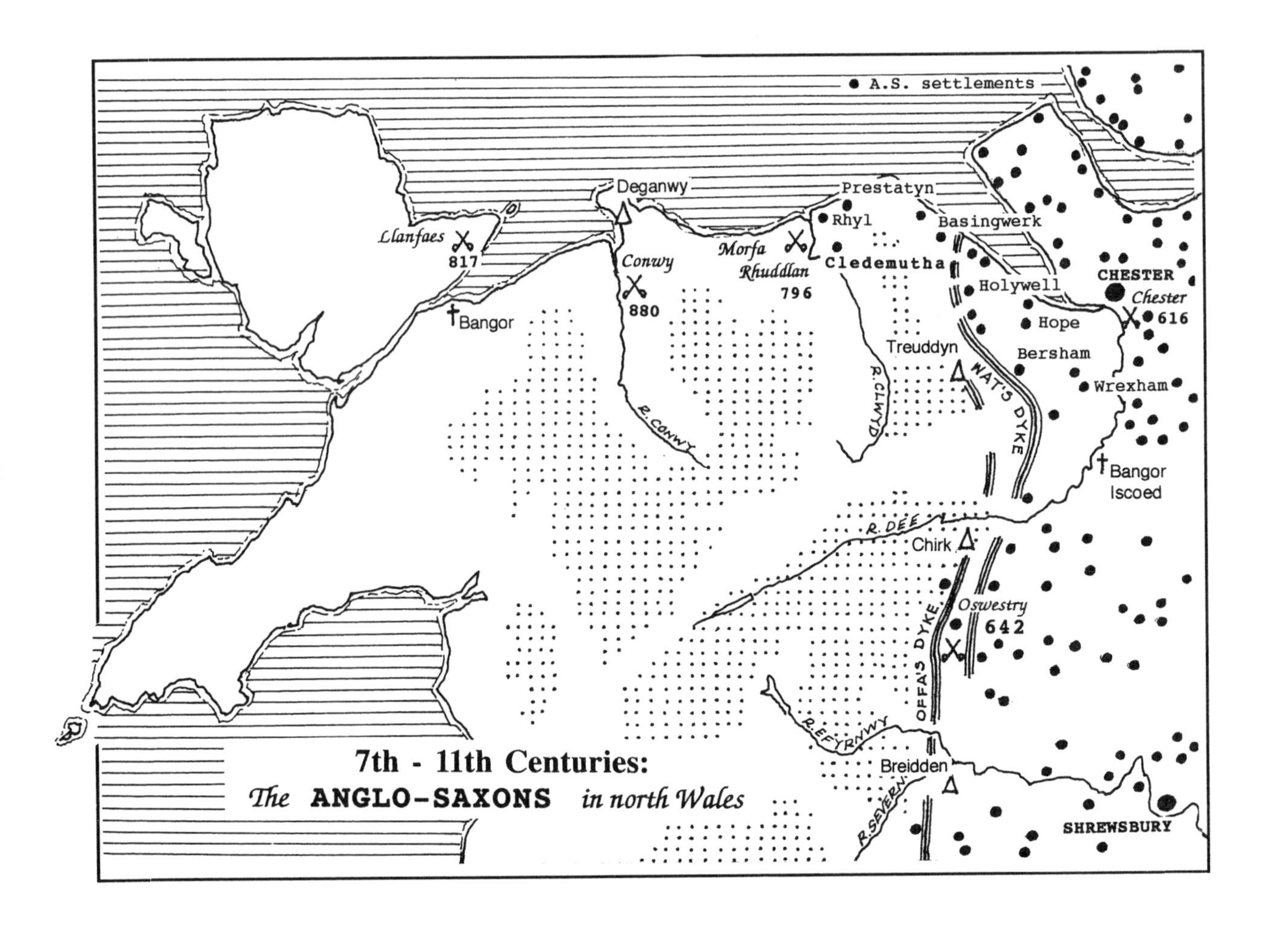

7th - 11th Centuries:
The **ANGLO-SAXONS** *in north Wales*

whom he also calls *Scotti*. He makes it clear, however, that they came to Britain from Ireland (*'Hibernia'*). He mentions Irish kingdoms in the Isle of Man, South Wales and Dal Riada. He then states that they were expelled from the whole of Britain by Cunedda and his sons.

The campaign of Cunedda against the invading Irish must have been a well-planned and long-drawn-out affair; indeed the usual addition 'and his sons' may indicate its span as several generations. It is probable, however, that 'and his sons' means together with his tribe, and we may see a large and close-knit group involved.

Nennius also specifies that Cunedda came to North Wales from Manaw Gododdin, the territory of the Gododdin, who had their capital at Edinburgh. We know of the Gododdin as a warlike tribe from an early poem, possibly the earliest poem of Britain, which commemorates the tribe's defeat at the battle of Catraeth, a battle which probably took place about 600 A.D. This, a sturdy epic of more than a thousand lines, strongly written and often moving, must be unique in literature as a tribal epic recording the defeat, rather than the victory, of its tribe.

Cunedda and his group of the Gododdin came to Wales some two hundred years before that fatal battle of Catraeth. The actual date of his coming is not recorded, but it must have been after the Roman withdrawal by Magnus Maximus in 383, and a date of about 400 seems likely.

What is significant about the coming of Cunedda, from our point of view, is that he founded the kingdom of Gwynedd. King Maelgwn, of whom we know much, traced his ancestry to Cunedda, and from this we may conjecture that their kingdoms were based in the same area. In the excavations of Maelgwn's citadel at Deganwy a short stretch of dry-stone walling was found which the archeologist, Leslie Alcock, thought might be as early as the second century, and a series of Roman coins of the third and fourth centuries also mean that there was some sort of fortification here at Deganwy even before Cunedda came to North Wales. He may then very well have founded his kingdom at the same spot as that later associated with the dynasty which he also founded.

We trace our history as a region to Cunedda. Without his arrival and success North Wales would certainly have become another Irish colony, like Dyfed in South Wales and Dal Riada in Scotland – indeed in the end like much of Scotland. There is evidence that it was a close-run thing. The Mabinogion story of 'Branwen' tells of Irish visits to Anglesey, where still hut circles such as those on Holyhead mountain are known as 'Cytiau Gwyddelod', the Irishmen's huts. The name of the Lleyn peninsula itself is Irish in origin, being related to Leinster, and indeed the name Gwynedd is said by some to come from the word 'Gwyddel', the name given to the Irish by the Welsh, which is related to the Irish 'Goidel' and to the words Gael and Gaelic.

Nennius says that the expulsion of the Irish by Cunedda took place 146 years before the reign of Maelgwn, his descendant. We do not know much about the years 400 to 546 in North Wales. Post-Roman finds such as 4th-century coins at Dinorben indicate a continued use of the hill forts. Into this gap, however, both Gildas and Nennius insert the complex figure of Vortigern, and Nennius specifically brings him to North Wales.

Gildas paints a grim picture of what things were like after the Roman withdrawal. The Scots and the Picts were savage and ruthless, and they overran the whole of the north of the country. The Roman towns were abandoned, and famine prevailed. In 446 (indicating that somebody was nevertheless still in charge) the Britons sent a letter to the Consul Aëtius, commander of the army of the western empire, begging for help, under the title 'the groans of the British'. It got no reply.

Maelgwn's fortress on the round hill above Deganwy is therefore completely explicable. It protected the coast, the river and its harbour against the hordes from the Irish Sea, the waters of which, if Gildas is right, must sometimes have been black with coracles. When Vortigern came to Snowdonia however he came in flight from a different threat, one so far unknown in this western political context.

Vortigern (which is probably a title rather than a name, like Caesar) was the high-king of Britain. Since this fact does not seem to have concerned the sons of Cunedda, who had their own dynasty and kingdom, we may view his territory as being based on the Roman province Britannia. It was threatened (as we know from Gildas) by the onslaughts of the Picts. To help him defend the province on several fronts he made an alliance with a group of Germanic colonists who had arrived in Kent. In exchange for land and supplies, they were to 'drive back the peoples of the north'. But they sent for their relatives and compatriots from Germany, and as their numbers increased the hard-pressed king was unable to keep up their demanded supplies.

What was he to do, when they rebelled? His council advised him to retreat, and probably he had no option. North Wales was still evidently regarded as safe, so he came to Gwynedd.

According to the Anglo-Saxon Chronicle that was in 449 A.D. The place he found most suitable for building a citadel was a hill below Snowdon, now called Dinas Emrys. When Dr Savory of the National Museum of Wales excavated Dinas Emrys in the years 1954-6 he found evidence of a substantial and luxurious settlement there in the second half of the fifth century. The early sources assure us, however, that that was not the court of Vortigern, but of his successor, Emrys, better known by his Roman name Ambrosius.

Welsh myth in fact associates this hilltop with both Vortigern and Ambrosius, though the latter is transformed into a prototype of the wizard Merlin. It was here, in the story, that the king confronted Emrys as a boy, and through the retelling of it by Geoffrey of Monmouth this precocious prophet became renamed Merlin.

History, archeology and mythology meet here on this mild and unassuming hill, in a rare coincidence of their essences. The story tells us that the fleeing king tried to build a castle, but the materials disappeared overnight. His wizards prescribed human sacrifice, specifically of a child with no father. This theme of child-sacrifice indicates a druidic, certainly pre-Christian tradition, so that the tale may be very old. We must remember that Nennius was working from the oral culture as well as written records.

Such a child is found and brought, but the boy, confronted with imminent destruction, proves to be prophetic. He knows more about the site than they do. He knows that under the surface of the hilltop is a pool, and that in the pool are two containers in which are sleeping dragons – literally, 'worms'. The worms then fight. The boy explains the symbolism of what takes place. The worms are emblematic dragons, the red one the native dragon, the white that of the invading nation. For a time the latter will appear to win, but later, he predicts, the native Britons will recover their strength and drive out the Germanic invaders.

Vortigern, however, must move on. The boy Emrys claimed the hilltop as his own. Vortigern, as it happens, is heard of again in story and in place-name, since his final retreat and place of death is said to be the steep-sided, almost unapproachable valley called after him, Nant Gwrtheyrn, which lies near the neck of the Lleyn peninsula. Bordered on one side by the sea and protected elsewhere by its sheer sides, this has always been a place of refuge. A burial chamber in its depths on a mound called Castell Gwrtheyrn was visible until about 1700, and naturally known as Bedd Gwrtheyrn, the grave of Vortigern. When the locals excavated it they found the bones of a tall man in a stone coffin.

That Vortigern existed is very probable, that is, that there was a high-king of Britain in the first half of the fifth century. We find a reference to him in the genealogy inscribed on a stone cross at the Abbey of Valle Crucis, near Llangollen, in which he is said to be the ancestor of the princes of Powys. It is not uncommon for princely houses to boost their status by tracing themselves back to early heroes, sometimes even to gods, and in fact this one also states that Vortigern was the son-in-law of Magnus Maximus, the Macsen of our previous chapter. What this inscription does prove, however, is that the character was known of and regarded as important at the time the pillar was inscribed, the early ninth century.

Gildas does not name him, but there is no doubt that the 'proud overlord' whom he blames for Britain's subsequent woes is the same man who is blamed, in less intemperate form, by Nennius. Gildas sees his successor (as Nennius does, but this time in fanciful terms) as Ambrosius. And there is no doubt also that Ambrosius existed. Gildas attributes to him the leadership of a campaign of resistance to the invaders which was for a time successful. We do not however have any evidence for connecting him to North Wales, apart from this one occurrence at Dinas Emrys.

Now that the hill and area of Dinas Emrys have been acquired by the National Trust, it is possible to view this primally historic site. You can see the marshy valley on top of the hill which is where the dragons were said to have been buried. Remarkably Dr Savory, in his excavations, found corroboration there of that highly symbolic tale: a platform had been built over the hollow, during the Dark Age occupation, and part of it apparently later removed.

The only visible ruins on Dinas Emrys now belong to the 13th century, when some unknown lord built a keep there, the tower of which still partly remains. The hill was, however, surrounded by a rampart, and this may be seen in places among the scrub oak which clothes the slopes. What is superb about Dinas Emrys is the view it affords, over Llyn Dinas to Nant Gwynant, a truly North Welsh view of a world of crags and peaks and native oak.

While Gildas blames Vortigern for initiating the post-Roman decline, the loss of Britain, he is eager to show also that the mistake had been aggravated rather than overcome by the behaviour of the kings who ruled after him. The fact that there were many at the same time cannot have helped. Britain was evidently no longer ruled by a high-king.

The number of courts of Dark Age Britain is rather surprisingly matched by their luxury. While a king of this period was living in some comfort at Dinas Emrys, another was living in positive decadence at Deganwy. Gildas and the archeologists agree about this: these local despots looked after themselves well.

'Why wallow like a fool in the ancient ink of your crimes, like a man drunk on wine pressed from the Sodomites vines?' thunders Gildas at Maelgwn, and sure enough we find the shards of imported wine jars at

Deganwy, Maelgwn's seat. How can a king of a small place like Gwynedd import wine from the Mediterranean in an age which we have labelled 'Dark'? No doubt we have been led by this misnomer into thinking of these people as primitive, when all that is deficient about them is our own state of knowledge of their times.

Gildas' urgency is made the more potent by the fact that he, but not Maelgwn, could see quite clearly what was coming. While the king indulged in his gross excesses on this western seabord, 'those fierce Saxons, of abominable name, hated by god and by men, are allowed into this island like wolves into a sheepfold'.

Gildas blames the disunity of the country and the low moral standards of its leaders. 'Britain has kings, but they are despots.' He catalogues their faults, then picks on them one by one. His tone is bitter and accusing, but when he comes to Maelgwn his anger is unmistakably heightened by pain. Clearly he knows the man personally. His anguish at the king's failure is made poignant by his knowledge that Maelgwn, amongst them all, had the qualities which, had he not corrupted them, could have led to success.

> You are last in my list but first in evil, stronger that many at once in power and wickedness, abundant in giving, profuse in sin, strong in arms, but stronger in the destruction of the soul, oh Maglocunus.

It need not have been so, he clearly tells us. Maelgwn's position and physique set him above the rest.

> The King of all Kings made you higher than almost all the leaders of Britain, in your kingdom as in your position, yet do you not show yourself to be morally worse than all the others, rather than better?

Certainly Maelgwn had power, as well as strength of character. The stories which have come down to us in later literature portray a dictatorial, violently-tempered man. Cleverer than the other petty kings, he lorded it over much of Wales. Hence, no doubt, the imported wine jars at Deganwy. From the later stories, as from Gildas, we can know him to have been a grossly self-indulgent man. He surrounded himself with flatterers, and, like so many autocrats, was only told what he wanted to hear.

Except by Gildas. Gildas' tone as well as his words make it clear that he was writing at the time, and expected Maelgwn to read him. His is the editorial in the opposition press. He speaks directly to his victim, with a fearlessness which may result from an old friendship. Yet he is not unrealistic enough to think that what he says will have any effect. 'You may hear this with deaf ears, rejecting the prophets, disparaging Christ, considering me, granted that I am of worthless quality, as of no importance.'

This, then, is one of the things which went wrong. Too many kings looked after their own sectional interests, and Maelgwn was the worst among them, at Deganwy, when he could have been the best.

There was very probably a deeper cause to the collapse than this personal one, though no-one should underestimate the effects of flaws or strengths of personality on the flow of history. If you stand on the Vardre above Deganwy today, where Maelgwn stood in the first half of the sixth century, and consider what you see, a visible fact comes home to you. He was facing the wrong way. For his father, grandfather and great-grandfather before him the threat had come from the Irish Sea. It came from there no longer, yet he sat in his castle here, drinking his fine wine and looking out to sea. The threat now came creeping from behind, and he could not see it. Across the broad midland plains it came, and into the Severn valley to the borders of his kingdom. And he didn't know.

He didn't know that by the year 547 (the year he died) the Anglian kingdoms of Deira and Bernicia had been established on the east coast for some seventy years, and were poised to become united as Northumbria. He didn't know that for more than a decade a Saxon kingdom had been expanding northwards from the Isle of Wight. A Jutish kingdom had been founded in Kent as early as the middle of the previous century, and it is even possible that he was unaware of this. By his time the foreign settlers had begun to move westwards up the river Trent.

Maelgwn himself died not in battle but of the yellow plague, an epidemic of which swept across Europe in the mid sixth century. The Welsh Annals record the year of his death as *'anno mortalitas magna'*, a year of great death. Once again the legend mirrors the history with appealing distortion. The story tells how the poet-prophet Taliesin had foretold that the king would be killed by a yellow monster, and that the fear of this so played on Maelgwn that he shut himself in the church at Llanrhos, near his castle at Deganwy. There in fear he looked through the keyhole, and saw the yellow monster approaching. The mere sight of it was enough to kill him. Presumably the more prosaic description of this is that he was already infected when he took refuge in the church.

Many other stories are told of Maelgwn, and although we only have them from a late 14th or early 15th century source they probably reflect the distorted memory of a real tradition. He appears to have been interested in music and poetry, and we know that he surrounded himself with flattering bards, since both the stories and Gildas say so. He was at least nominally a Christian, as were all the British kings (and none, at this date, of the Germanic ones). He had a short temper and was high-handed and intolerant. From one source or another we know a surprising amount about him.

Leslie Alcock's excavations on the Vardre at Deganwy, Maelgwn's seat, took place during the years 1961-66 over a total of fourteen weeks, being sponsored by the Board of Celtic Studies of the University of Wales. He found mainly items from the later periods of the site's use, which we shall encounter again. The dozen or so pieces of wine jar however speak volumes, not only about Maelgwn but about the general conditions of the time. We already know it was an age of epic poetry and heroic standards, and now the wine jars tells us it was also an age of a certain internationalism and capacity for trade.

These sherds of amphorae are of special interest because they can be fairly accurately assigned. They came from the eastern Mediterranean and were made in the late fifth or during the sixth century. They are known from a number of other 'Dark Age' sites in Britain, and in fact are classified as 'Tintagel class B'.

It is interesting to wonder what Deganwy had to offer the eastern Mediterranean in exchange.

The lack of other finds at Deganwy from this period is surprising, and unusual for such a site. Leslie Alcock speculates that it might be an indication of a sophisticated settlement rather than a poor one. The more developed the court, he argues (in Geoffrey Ashe's book, 'The Quest for Arthur's Britain'), 'the greater the cleanliness observed, and the less the archeologically interesting filth that is littered around.'

While the Vardre and Dinas Emrys were the main sites occupied in North Wales in post-Roman times, they were by no means the only ones. There are signs that several Iron Age forts were reoccupied at this period, and in 1954 an excavation at Garn Boduan on the Lleyn peninsula (a large and impressive hillfort with the remains of a great many huts) found a small post-Roman fortification occupying nearly half an acre of the hilltop. The name associates the place with Buan, a contemporary of Maelgwn, and perhaps indicates a limit to Maelgwn's power or the extent of his territory.

There is evidence that the Iron Age fort at Dinorben was also refortified and occupied in the sixth century, as were such forts in other parts of Britain. In this we may see a response to an emerging threat, perhaps the time when the aftermath of the *pax Romana* (which had allowed trade with the Mediterranean and no doubt facilitated the import of wine) was coming to an end, and a nation unused to war was having to defend itself. In this we may see a renewal of the Irish threat or marauders coming down the Irish Sea from Scotland.

One notable innovation, and one with which Maelgwn Gwynedd is closely associated, is the coming, at this time, of Christianity. It is asserted by Gildas that Maelgwn was educated by 'the refined master of almost all Britain'. Later tradition holds that both Gildas and Maelgwn were taught by St Illtud, who founded a monastery in South Wales in the early sixth century. That Maelgwn was a Christian is not in doubt, and tradition then shows him as the benefactor, by the grant of land, of many monasteries. For instance, he gave the Roman fort at Holyhead to St Cybi, in about 540, which explains why the parish church is right in the middle of the Roman enclosure. Since the same thing has happened at Caerhun, where the church sits in the middle of the remains of Canovium, the influence of Maelgwn may have been felt there too, and the modern name commemorates his son, Rhun – Caerhun meaning 'the fort of Rhun'.

It is remarkable to think how early in time Christianity came to North Wales. The English were not converted until the mission of St Augustine in Kent in the 590's, and even then it was a largely nominal and limited conversion. Yet while St Cybi was established with royal approval at Caergybi, St Seiriol set up his church on the other side of Anglesey, at Penmon, also an area where Maelgwn is said to have shown an interest.

Although the church at Holyhead dates from the 15th and 16th centuries, and the monastic buildings at Penmon Priory from the 13th onwards, there remains at Penmon one remnant of these early Christian foundations of the 540's and the reign of Maelgwn, in the form of the foundations of a small cell, looking much like an Iron Age hut circle, in which the saint very probably lived. Nearby is St Seiriol's well, covered by a small chapel building, its spring issuing the water with which he baptised his flock.

The map of North Wales today is dotted with the 'llans' of these sixth century saints. One such was Tudno, who founded his community on the Great Orme, where a church dedicated to him still stands, though of course his wattle cell has long ago gone; and his name lives on as that of Wales' foremost seaside town, the resort of Llandudno which stretches on the plain below his hilltop settlement. Each of these saints was given a later 'Life', in which they are fitted out with background details, and Tudno was said to have been the son of a courtier from Cantref Gwaelod, an inundated area off the southern Gwynedd coast.

In reality, as opposed to hagiography, all these clerics were part of a movement which also led to the founding of St Columba's monastery on Iona. As a whole they were an evangelical community, in the sense of

39 *Dinas Brân, above Llangollen, is an example of an early Welsh castle which later fell into the possession of a marcher lord.*

40 *The castle at Cricieth was originally built by Llywelyn the Great in the 1230's*

41 *Dolwyddelan castle is traditionally the birthplace of Llywelyn the Great but was probably built by him.*

42 *Dolbadarn was built by Llywelyn in about 1230, and introduces a new style of circular tower in place of the square keep.*

43 *Ewloe was one of the earliest of the Welsh castles, possibly first built by Owain Gwynedd and later developed by his grandson Llywelyn the Great.*

44 *Tomen y Rhodwydd, near Llandegla, was built by Owain Gwynedd in 1148.*

45 *The stone coffin of Princess Joan still stands*

46 *The base of the sarcophagus of Llywelyn the Great is in the Gwydir chapel adjoining Llanrwst church.*

47 *The old church of Llanrhychwyn in the hills above Trefriw was replaced by the parish church in the valley during the reign of Llywelyn the Great. Parts of it date from the time of his grandfather Owain Gwynedd, the second half of the 12th century.*

48 *The final war was started when Prince Llywelyn's brother Dafydd attacked Hawarden castle, then an English stronghold.*

49 *Flint was the first new castle to be built by Edward I in northern Wales.*

50 *Edward improved the castle at Rhuddlan which had originally been a seat of the Marcher lords.*

51 *Llywelyn's hall at Conwy was incorporated into the town wall by Edward I, and is still identifiable by its windows in the tower and the wall.*

52 *Caernarfon castle was in the early stages of being built when the future Edward II was born there, in April 1284.*

53 *The Statute of Rhuddlan imposed on the newly conquered areas of northern Wales the English county administration and the English legal system.*

54 *In 1283 Edward called a Parliament at Rhuddlan, at a site in the main street known as 'Parliament Building'.*

55 *As soon as he had taken the west bank of the Conwy, Edward set about defending the crossing and the harbour by constructing Conwy castle and walled town, in 1284.*

having a mission to convert, to spread the religion and to minister to its new believers.

St Columba himself came from Ireland to Iona with a number of monks in 563. By then, however, Cadoc and David, and Gildas himself, had been busy establishing churches in Wales for half a century. What Iona did was set up a permanent base and reference point for British Christians, and a structured monastic regime.

It is important in this that Columba's religious system was based on the monastic, rather than the diocesan, form. Abbots were superior to Bishops, and the effect of this was to make the seat of power the local group, the community itself, rather than a distant, hierarchical, central church. Geoffrey Ashe, in his seminal book 'From Caesar to Arthur', points out that this was only possible because Scotland and Ireland had never been part of the Roman Empire. North Wales, though at least partly Romanised, benefited from the freedom of its neighbours by being Christianised by them before the Rome-based, church-dominated version brought by St Augustine reached it. There is much in its subsequent history and present-day attitude that is due to this chance.

The difference in style and approach between the two versions of the same religion has run through our history, and today it still marks an identity, in terms of values and beliefs, which distinguishes Wales. In particular it gave rise to a form of religion which, because community-based and not reliant on a superior authority, was better adaptable to local social change. It would not be too far-fetched to see the trend towards democratisation of the law ultimately enshrined in the early Tudor reforms (such as for instance the use of lay magistrates, the J.P. system) as being the outcome of these democratic principles.

As we remarked in an earlier chapter, the type of Non-Conformism so prevalent in North Wales is the present-day expression of a social attitude which resisted central doctrine; St Columba's style of monastic Christianity fitted perfectly with this approach.

St Illtud, a figure of the sixth century, was not only traditionally the teacher of Maelgwn and Gildas, but also of St David. He is said in the Saints Lives to have served in the army, and if so it may well have been under Ambrosius, thus linking this post-Roman world to its Roman roots. Of the saints more directly connected to North Wales, we have already mentioned Cybi, Seiriol and Tudno. St Cadfan is another early North Welsh saint, notable for having founded the monastery on Bardsey Island, which became a refuge for ecclesiastics in the troubled centuries ahead, and through that, as the reputed burial place of 20,000 saints, a place of pilgrimage during the Middle Ages.

St Collen, founder of Llangollen, illustrates the mobility which was so characteristic of this missionary movement. At work during the seventh century, he moved from Ireland to Britain, to France, to southern England and then to Glastonbury, where he became Abbot. From there in due course he moved to Llangollen, founding the church there, and there he ended his days.

Almost all the churches which now bear the names of these saints were founded in the sixth century. Nothing of course of those original structures survives. Churches were not built in stone until the twelfth century, and many of North Wales' churches date in part at least from then. Originally they were small cells of wattle-and-daub. Nevertheless the fine and sturdy churches in these parishes of North Wales today undoubtedly enclose the spots originally made holy by those early missionaries, as is made explicit at St Beuno's church of Clynnog Fawr on the pilgrim route down the Lleyn peninsula, where the saint himself is said to be buried.

One striking innovation which these early Christians caused, which is highly relevant to our purpose here, is the use of writing.

Whether or not they were influenced by the descended wisdom of the druids, they did not share the druidic superstition which forbade written records. St Illtud, said by both Gildas and the writer of his 'Life' to be the wisest and most learned man in Britain was said also to be a wise man by descent, and a druid, from which we may suppose that he was a member of a priestly class. Because of this connection with their predecessors these new priests had access to the inherited lore and wisdom which it was the privilege of their class to bear and transmit. To our great good fortune they combined the new medium of writing with that old material. They wrote it down.

Thus we have the Welsh Annals to refer to. We are no longer dependant, from the sixth century, on Roman historians. Thus too we have Nennius, already much referred to, writing in Bangor in North Wales in about 800 A.D., and so quite near to the period he was dealing with. They wrote in Latin, which was the language of the international church. When we finally get news of our early history in the native language, in the *'Brut y Tywysogion'*, the 13th century 'Chronicle of the Princes', it is in the form of a contemporary translation of a lost Latin original.

The reign of Maelgwn came to an end in 547, and he was succeeded by his son Rhun. The latter was later reputed to have led an expedition against the British of the north, echoing Gildas' earlier complaint that internal wars continued after invasions had stopped.

External trouble, however, was by no means at an end. Indeed so much has this area subsequently been invaded that it is remarkable that it retains, as it undoubtedly does, so strong an individual identity. Maelgwn's ancestors had succeeded in quietening the Irish problem. His son appears to have had to deal with competition from fellow-Britons. It was their immediate descendants who had to take on the biggest threat of all, that of the emerging kingdoms of the Angles and Saxons, the subject of the next chapter.

Gildas is said in the Welsh Annals to have died in 570. If so, he did not himself witness the worst of the outcome of the catastrophic mistakes which he identified. He was aware, evidently by the time he wrote his book, that the Saxons had overrun much of the rest of Britain. It was only early in the seventh century that their impact began to be felt in North Wales.

By the time Nennius was compiling his 'heap' in Bangor in about 800, North Wales had been through its brief, and only, period of independence and relative peace, and was by then thoroughly embroiled again in dealing with outsiders. It was during that period that the Celtic missionaries founded their monastic churches and thus planted the roots of something which evidently flourishes well in Welsh soil. A story is told of one of them which poignantly describes the coming end of their brief idyll.

St Beuno was the founder of several churches. During his time at the end of the sixth and start of the seventh centuries he brought Christianity to the western tips of North Wales, and as has been mentioned churches bearing his name now stand at Clynnog Fawr, and also at Pistyll, on the Lleyn peninsula. Originally he came from Mid Wales, and later in his career he returned to Powys and was granted land in what is now Shropshire by the king of Powys.

One day Beuno was walking by the river Severn with one of his disciples. Across the river they heard a strange sound. A huntsman was calling to his dogs. It was not the cry of hunting that was strange, but that it occurred in a language they had never heard before.

Up the rivers they had come, spreading. The Ouse and the Derwent brought them out of Northumbria, until they met the Trent. The Trent carried them south and north into the Midlands, where eventually they found themselves on the eastern bank of the Severn. It was almost certainly Anglian, not Saxon, that Beuno and his colleague heard. The hunting party was the vanguard of the Anglian kingdom which was in due course to become Mercia.

Bibliography

Gildas, *The Ruin of Britain*, trs. Michael Winterbottom, Phillimore.
Nennius, *British History and The Welsh Annals*, trs. John Morris, Phillimore.
Aneirin, *Y Gododdin*, A.O.H. Jarman. Gomer Press.
Arthur's Britain. Leslie Alcock, Penguin.
From Caesar to Arthur. Geoffrey Ashe. Collins.
The Quest for Arthur's Britain. Geoffrey Ashe. Pall Mall.
Welsh Christian Origins. A.W. Wade-Evans. Alden.

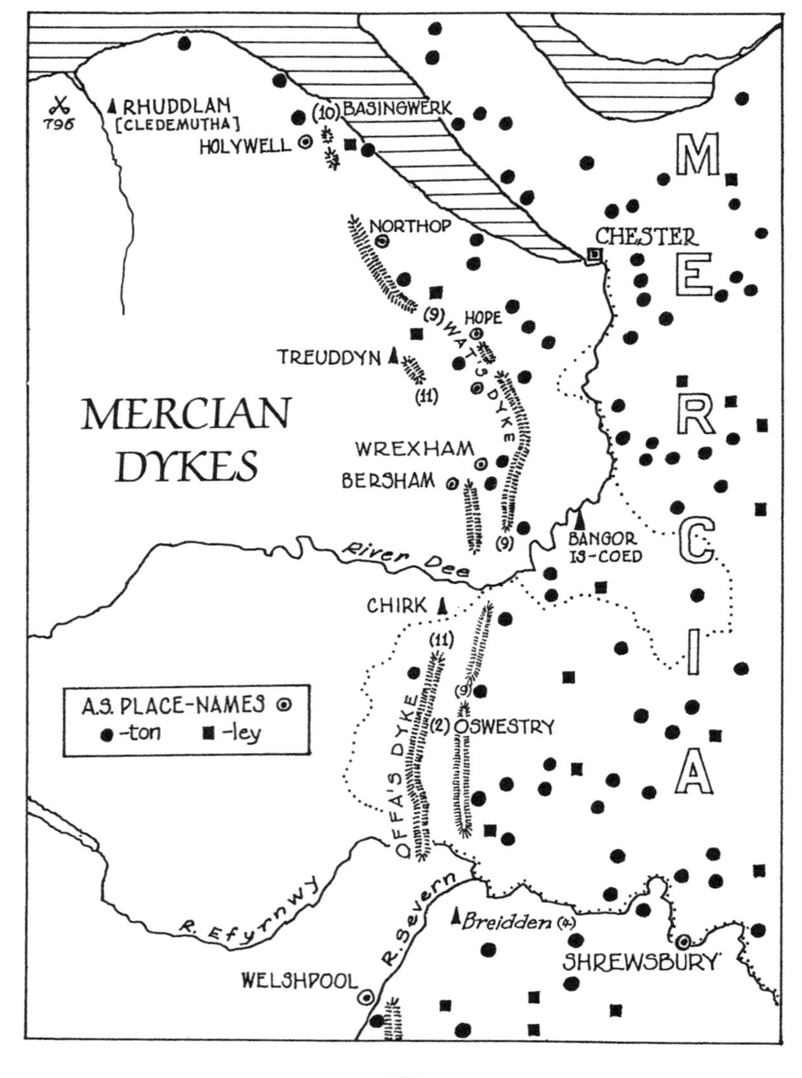

Allies and Enemies

'These new-comers were from the three most formidable races of Germany, the Saxons, Angles, and Jutes. From the Jutes are descended the people of Kent and the Isle of Wight and those in the province of the West Saxons opposite the Isle of Wight who are called Jutes to this day. From the Saxons – that is, the country now known as the land of the Old Saxons – came the East, South and West Saxons. And from the Angles – that is, the country known as Angulus, which lies between the provinces of the Jutes and Saxons and is said to remain unpopulated to this day – are descended the East and Middle Angles, the Mercians, all the Northumbrian stock (that is, those people living north of the river Humber), and the other English peoples.'

So Bede, writing in the 730's, laid down the basis of our official view of the formation of England. Much of the time Bede was working directly from Gildas, but this passage seems to have come from another source. Indeed the contrast which it bears to Bede's normally fluent style has suggested to some that it was a last-minute insertion, information of which he had only just been made aware. It is generally accepted to be as near to an accurate picture as we are going to get for a situation which was to say the least confused. The confusion remains with us to this day, when the Scots and the Welsh still term 'Saxons' the people who are known to themselves as the English.

Ironically as far as North Wales was concerned there was little direct involvement with the Saxons themselves. The people whom the kings of North Wales came into contact with, both, as we shall see, as allies and as enemies, were Angles. Bede's analysis brings home to us one thing: there was great disparity among the invading groups. Indeed history bears this out, since they spent the first few hundred years in our island fighting each other. What is slightly more surprising is that we get conflict even within the groups themselves, and North Wales' position meant that it was a party to the rivalry between the Angles of Northumbria and the Angles of Mercia.

The kingdoms of Bernicia and Deira (roughly speaking Yorkshire and the present Durham and Northumberland) united under Aethelfrith in

604 to become the kingdom of Northumbria, which had developed into the dominant force in northern Britain long before the rise of Mercia under Penda in the 620's. For a long time the independent British kingdoms of Gwynedd and Powys remained protected from the aggressive might of Northumbria by the northern British kingdoms of Rheged and Gododdin. These, while they were powerful, acted as a buffer to constrain Northumbrian ambition. It was the sudden downfall of each of these which released the monster.

The northern Anglian kingdoms (Bernicia and Deira) had already been allowed to expand, however, by the end of the sixth century, by the weakening of these two British kingdoms. Urien of Rheged had almost beaten the incipient Northumbrians into the sea, in 577; but in doing so he met his death. While he had the enemy besieged on the island of Lindisfarne he was betrayed by one of his own followers, who murdered him out of jealousy. The Angles took advantage of the loss of this major leader and seized further British territory. Moreover the attempt by the Gododdin to recover this ended in a further, crucial disaster.

In about 600 the king of the Gododdin assembled a force from many British kingdoms and launched an attack on the town of Catraeth, modern Catterick in Yorkshire, which lay at the joining point of the allied nations of Deira and Bernicia, soon to become Northumbria.

The expedition was a disastrous failure. The crack force of three hundred horsemen was almost exterminated, and of the much larger band which historians suppose would have accompanied them almost none returned. What was to have been the native Britons' revival proved their sudden and comprehensive decline.

After the amalgamation of Deira and Bernicia, which these events permitted, there was no containing the imperialistic aspirations of the new Northumbria. By 613 Aethelfrith arrived as far south as Powys, and shortly after that he reached the Irish Sea.

It was not however only the Welsh who were threatened by this expansion.

The kingdom of Mercia had come into being by gradual degrees. First, Anglian settlers had arrived in Cheshire, where the land suited their type of agriculture. They had a developed arable system at a time when the Welsh were mainly stock farmers, and the Roman clearances on the Cheshire plain were ideal for their purposes. This sort of farming led to a clearly identifiable form of settlement, in which the dwellings are grouped close to the worked land. Stock farming, however, involves a wider spread of habitation. We can see the results of this variation in characteristic of settlement pattern clearly today, when many a rural

Welsh township is not what one would think of as a village at all, but rather a wide spread of scattered farms; whereas on and around the English border are those neat little conformations of closely-packed cottages. It was settlements of this kind that had begun, by the end of the sixth and the start of the seventh century, to develop into the kingdom of Mercia.

When Aethelfrith of Bernicia amalgamated the two countries to form Northumbria, Edwin, the heir of Deira, still an infant, was hurried by his people into exile. Cadfan, king of Gwynedd, gave him refuge at his court of Aberffraw in Anglesey, where he was brought up with Cadfan's son Cadwallon. Later tales picture them racing their horses against each other on Aberffraw's beach.

There are a number of interesting points about this. Cadfan was evidently a notable king. An inscription on a stone in the church of Llangadwaladr in Anglesey records his fame. Once used as a lintel for the south door, it is now fixed into a wall. Undoubtedly this is Cadfan's epitaph, and it speaks highly of him:

CATAMANUS
REX SAPIENTISI
MUS OPINATISIM
MUS OMNIUM REG
UM

'King Cataman, wisest and most renowned of all kings'.

The blithe disregard for spacing which leaves words ending on the next line is common in early inscriptions, and indeed in comparatively modern ones. The lettering is interesting, and seems to make the work contemporary with the king it praises. The N's are written like H's, the U's squared at the bottoms, and the M's are three parallel vertical lines touching each other at a bulge in the middle. The wording too is interesting, and marks the writer as British rather than continental. The use of the word 'opinatus' in the sense of 'illustrious' instead of its more usual meaning, 'conjectured', has a Biblical comparison, and so may make the composer of this grand phrase a churchman familiar with the Latin Bible. Most interesting of all is the suggestion that Cadfan was better than all other kings, meaning perhaps that he held a sort of high-kingship within Wales.

Cadfan was the son of Iago, who was the son of Beli, who was the son of Rhun the son of Maelgwn: great-great grandson of Maelgwn Gwynedd, and so a man of high nobility. The line indeed went on from him, to produce the ruling princes of Wales. It was his grandson,

Cadwaladr, who founded the church in which his epitaph now resides.

Since the stories mention Edwin as having been raised at Cadfan's court at Aberffraw, it seems as if the seat of the kings of Gwynedd had by the early seventh century moved from Deganwy to Anglesey, where, as we shall see, it was to stay. Aberffraw is now a modest and peaceful place on the attractive western coast, but for several hundred years it was the centre of considerable power.

When Edwin grew up his thoughts turned to his lost kingdom, and he moved east into Cheshire. There he found the settlers beginning to organise themselves politically, to the extent even of having a king, Ceorl, whose daughter he prudently married. Thus Edwin of Deira was allied to the Mercians, and to consolidate this base he also began to negotiate with the East Angles.

What understandably frightened Aethelfrith was the thought of this continuous power-block forming on his southern border, all the way from the east coast to the Irish Sea. He saw that he had to split the Angles from the Welsh. He marched his army south-west, towards their joining point.

The Battle of Chester, which then took place (in 616 or 617 A.D.), is normally represented as being between the English and the Welsh, and one which the English won. This is wrong on both counts. It was in fact at root an internal conflict between the two houses of Northumbria, those of Deira and Bernicia, and contingently directed against a Mercian-Welsh alliance. It was a battle as much between Angles and Angles as between English and Welsh.

Moreover it would also be simplistic to say that the English won it, because in a sense everybody seems to have lost. One feature of the battle which was significant was that Aethelfrith had arrived so quickly and unexpectedly that a main part of the Welsh army was not there at all. Cadfan and the army of Gwynedd arrived after the battle was over. He had the honour of pursuing the retreating army. Much damage had already been done on both sides by then.

The army of the king of Powys, Selyf, was nearer to the scene, and so took the initial assault. A troop from eastern Gwynedd supported them. To bulk out this rather thin defending force the Welsh called on the monks of the nearby monastery of Bangor-on-Dee, or more correctly, in its Welsh form, Bangor-is-y-coed. J.D. Bu'lock, whose 'Pre-Conquest Cheshire' forms a main secondary source for this event, points out that the use of monks in battle is not as bizzare as it might seem, since monasteries were the retirement homes of warriors, and that at Bangor probably counted former kings of Gwynedd and Powys among its brothers. As it happened their eminence and experience was not enough, and they should have stayed in retirement. Aethelfrith massacred the monks. Over a thousand of them died.

With them fell a large number of the men of Powys (relegating that kingdom to a position of weakness for several generations) and the Northumbrian victory should have been secure. But their losses had been heavy too, and instead of consolidating their hold on Cheshire they then fled in front of Cadfan's arriving army. They went home, or rather they set out to do so. The journey involved passing through consistently hostile country. First Mercia, then the edge of the territory of the East Angles. It was the latter which decided the issue, by ambushing Aethelfrith's army near Bawtry in Yorkshire. They killed the retreated king and put his rival Edwin on the throne of Northumbria. Some victory, one may feel.

What is significant about this state of affairs, for us, is the effect it had on Edwin. Now king of the largest power-group yet to form in Britain, he turned, rather puzzlingly, on his former allies, in fact on his foster-brother himself.

Of this group of characterful leaders Edwin is the hardest for us to understand. Most notably he had every reason to be grateful to the house of Gwynedd, and anyone brought up on the pleasant shores of Anglesey must have at least a little nostalgia for the western Welsh ethos, a little appreciation for the independent attitude and enviable way of life of the Gwynedd kings. Perhaps he lost those horse-races, but it was a long time ago. It is of course possible that he and Cadwallon had always disliked each other, Edwin being in an expatriate position at the court of a king in which the young prince had a future of some easy certainty, as well as a greatly illustrious family past, by contrast with his own slight dynastic background and unpropitious future. Though history overtly turns on strategy and power, we should never forget that its course is in the hands of human beings with personal strengths and fallibilities.

What we know is that the immediate succession of events is both strange and crucial. Clearly something in the meantime had been building up. Most likely Edwin resented his forced exile into Gwynedd, and determined that such things would never happen to him again. Then suddenly he saw the means being opened to him to ensure this. He saw that Northumbria could be so powerful as to be safe. He saw that its only threat lay in the latent power of the kingdom whose wealth and ability he knew so well. He reckoned without the rise of Mercia. What he knew was that Gwynedd was a potential threat.

Cadwallon had succeeded Cadfan in 625. Early in the 630's Edwin attacked his kingdom. He seems to have made a remarkably effective assault on Gwynedd, since its king was forced to retreat first into

Anglesey, then to its offshore islet, 'Puffin Island', or Priestholm, where he was for a time besieged, and finally into exile in Ireland. The kingdom of Northumbria then stretched right across Britain, from sea to sea.

This was not an acceptable situation for either the Welsh or the other Anglo-Saxons kingdoms. Cadwallon from Ireland was able to work on the rivalry between the invaders to bring about his own restoration to power. The West Saxons for instance had tried to have Edwin assassinated and for a time kept him busy attempting to put them in their place. It was to Mercia, however, the natural ally of Gwynedd rather than its enemy, that Cadwallon turned.

If Edwin was to keep his distant rivals the West Saxons under control he needed the help of Mercia. This now had a new king, Penda, the son of King Pebba who had built up a position of power and extended his country through the Midlands. For a time he seems to have acted as Edwin's agent in his contest with the West Saxons. Northumbria was not however to have things so easy for long. When Cadwallon came back from exile in 633 it was as part of an anti-Edwin faction, a coalition of Gwynedd and Mercia.

Penda had reasons to be afraid of Edwin's power. It is more than likely that his own extension of his kingdom northwards was a response to the threat of Edwin's covert intentions regarding Mercia. Penda had no reason to like or trust Edwin. He could also see that the interests of his country in this respect were identical to those of Gwynedd. As long as Gwynedd and Mercia worked together both were safe.

This was a powerful grouping and it spelt the end of Edwin. The two great kings, the Angle and the Welshman, led an army against him which produced his defeat and death, at Doncaster, on 14th October 633. His son was killed in the same battle, and the loss of them both left Northumbria in disorder.

For a year the kings of Gwynedd and Mercia ravaged Northumbria. The Christian missionary who had arrived in the recently stable country to convert its people fled, ironically, before these kings, one of whom was supposed to be a fellow-Christian. Bede says that Penda was a pagan but, with understandable distaste, blames Cadwallon, 'who called himself a Christian', for the atrocities which then took place. He spared neither women nor children. He showed no respect for religion. He was more savage than any pagan. He was utterly barbarous in temperament and in behaviour.

Here clearly we have a story involving two very different people. The one, Penda, brought to the situation the impetus of the newcomer's need for quick advancement. His kingdom was a mere generation old. His father, Pebba, had built it by expansion from its roots in modest settlements flourishing on a promising terrain. He was, it seems, both a careful diplomat and an arch pragmatist. His distrust of, and presumably dislike of, Edwin, provided a powerful personal motivation. But above all he was motivated by a need to establish his new-found power base, a need for the security which would allow him the brief time in which to build within it political cohesion. This he achieved, and duly Mercia blossomed, in the following decades, to become for a time the main force in Britain. It was his perception of the use to which alliance with Gwynedd could be put that facilitated this.

Clearly he saw strength in collaboration with Cadwallon, or he would not have worked so closely with someone who might have been regarded as a rival. He had to work with him for some time in the anti-Edwin league. Yet the two men could hardly have been more different. Cadwallon, a nominal Christian, and yet hot-blooded and bitter; Penda, worshipping Germanic gods yet politically sophisticated and apparently humane. How did they reconcile their religious and personal differences? When they negotiated and then campaigned together, what language, for instance, did they speak? It is hard to imagine either of them learning the other's tongue. To what extent, we wonder, did they really respect each other, the one an upstart king invading British soil, the other bearing the ancient blood of the house of Gwynedd.

One can see Bede's dilemma; he is writing a history of the church, and would naturally favour the Christian, in his report, against the pagan. Yet he is writing from an Anglian point of view, and in this case the Christian is Welsh. Penda comes out of it better, but one cannot imagine anyone emerging blameless from that one climactic year, 633.

At the end of that time however a new king emerged to rally the forces of Northumbria: Oswald, whose distinguished reign was to have much effect on the history of North Wales.

Oswald appeared apparently from nowhere in the chaotic situation in Northumbria, and at once became its king. He must have been a powerful leader. He was in fact a younger son of the great king Aethelfrith, whom we have met before as the instigator of the raid on North Wales which culminated in the Battle of Chester. During Edwin's supremacy he and his brothers had been in exile in Scotland. We must suppose that they hastened from there on the news of Edwin's death. His elder brothers however were killed during that year by Cadwallon, so that he was now the heir to the throne of Bernicia.

With Oswald Bede's dilemma is resolved. Here at last is an Angle and a good Christian. Oswald had learnt his Christianity in Scotland, so that it was of the Celtic variety. His elder brothers had lapsed from their beliefs before meeting their destiny at the hands of Cadwallon, but Oswald remained true to the church. Consequently Bede gives him ample space, and so we know quite a lot about the man who now became the main enemy of North Wales.

His first contact with Gwynedd was the defeat and execution of its king, the much-feared Cadwallon. Oswald caught up with him at a place afterwards called 'Heavenfield', near Hexham in the Tyne valley. Here Oswald defeated and personally killed Cadwallon of Gwynedd (who, if Bede is to be believed, was the equivalent of a war criminal), but for a time he left Penda of Mercia alone, presumably in exchange for help against the Saxons. This was rash, since in no time at all Penda had renewed his alliance with Gwynedd. In 642 it was necessary for Oswald to march south with his army to split this fatal coalition.

Oswald confronted the joint forces of Gwynedd, Powys and Mercia at a place known as Maserfeld, which we know from other evidence was at or near Oswestry. The allied forces were too much for him, and at Maserfeld he died: on 5th August, 642, Bede tells us, at the age of 38, after a reign of eight years.

The connection of Oswald's death with Oswestry relies on the name, since Oswestry is credibly derived from 'Oswald's Tree', referring to the cross which was set up to commemorate his death. Although this seems almost certain to be a correct interpretation it is odd that there is no mention of it until 1254, when we find a documentary reference to Croes Oswallt, 'Oswald's Cross'. Bede does not help us with the location of Maserfeld, though he tells of several miracles which later occurred there.

The immediate results of the defeat and death of Oswald led to a change in political balance in Britain which had crucial and long-term effects on North Wales. It is only when Mercia ceased to be an ally and became a threat that we can think in the terms to which we have been erroneously conditioned, the struggle of the native Welsh against the English settlers. For the first hundred years of the occupation this was not the case.

Penda of Mercia was a survivor. He had kept his life and his kingdom through the reigns of Edwin and Oswald, and seen his ally Cadwallon fall. According to one chronicler he fled to Brittany when Cadwallon was defeated, but this seems an unlikely course. If he fled anywhere it would be probably be into North Wales. In any case he returned in might.

After Oswestry Penda once again came into his own. Again he was in Northumbria causing havoc, this time without the help of the dreaded Cadwallon but nevertheless accompanied by his allies from North Wales.

They got as far as the ancient capital of Bamburgh. The new king, Oswiu, tried to bribe him to go home, but he refused, and a battle took place, this time of Angle against Angle but also of Christian against pagan, since Penda had still not accepted the faith. God won the day for Oswiu, who pursued Penda (now deserted by the Welsh) as far as Leeds and killed him there. He then ruled Mercia as well as Northumbria for the next three years, controlling a remarkable kingdom which even included some of Scotland. Wales did not escape his attention, and he began to penetrate his forces into Powys, where some of the arable country of the Shropshire plain, formerly in Welsh hands, became English then for ever.

Eryr Pengwern penngard llwyt heno
aruchel y euan
eidic am gic Kynndylan.

'The grey-crested eagle of Shrewsbury, its call high tonight, is eager for the flesh of Cynddylan' – evidently a Powys chieftain whose territory of Pengwern (Shrewsbury) was lost to Oswiu. So laments the contemporary bard.

Oswiu married his daughter to Penda's son, whom he allowed to rule the area of southern Mercia south of the river Trent. At this time Mercia became Christian, and paganism was finally ended as an official religion in Britain.

In the process of Oswiu's rise to domination the crucial Mercian-Welsh alliance had been destroyed, and when Mercia eventually returned to independence it was as a rival and primary threat to North Wales. It seems that Northumbria had overexpanded, and that Oswiu was unable to keep control of so many widespread provinces. Under the new Mercian kings Wulhere and then Aethelred (both sons of Penda) the ambitions of Northumbria were constantly challenged and restrained, and marriage of the latter to another of Oswiu's daughters did not succeed in achieving peace. This however was to be done by the intervention of the Archbishop of Canterbury, Theodore, but it had to await the death of Oswiu, in 670, and in fact followed a battle between Aethelred and Oswiu's successor Ecgfrith in 675. Theodore then intervened and successfully brokered peace.

It was this peace, which lasted for the next thirty-five years, which allowed the development of Mercia as a country not reliant on any deals with Wales. It was the constant rivalry between Mercia and Northumbria which had kept peace between the Welsh and Mercians until then. After 675 Mercia concerned itself more with its southern borders, and the dissolution into disorder of the leadership of Northumbria added to its stability and establishment of dominance in Britain.

The rise of Mercia was accompanied by a decline in the power and influence of the kingdoms which formed North Wales. Powys had sunk into decline with the defeat of its king, Selyf, son of the more powerful Cynan, at the Battle of Chester in 617. The kingdom of Gwynedd, under the rule of the descendants of Maelgwn, remained a powerful force until the death of Cadwallon at the hands of Oswald in 634. Thereafter Penda had maintained a puppet king of Gwynedd, Cadafael, a usurper whom he had placed on the throne, who was, however, to desert him at the crucial time of his pursuit by Oswiu. It is presumed that in the meantime the rightful king of Gwynedd, Cadwaladr, son of Cadwallon and grandson of Cadfan, had died. This however does not tally with the date given in the Welsh Annals, since Cadafael was with Penda in Northumbria in 655 and the Annals say that Cadwaladr died in 682, in a great plague which swept Britain. Perhaps, then, there were two kings of Gwynedd at that time, a rightful one and a usurper. We have to admit that this is a hazy area of history.

Cadwaladr for some reason gained a reputation in later lore much greater than would seem to be explained by his known activity. The one thing which is known of him for certain is that he founded the church in Anglesey already mentioned as being the site of his grandfather's memorial. The church there today is mainly a 17th century building, based on a mainly 14th century plan and largely rebuilt in the last century. It contains some fine late 15th century stained glass.

The second half of the seventh and first half of the eighth centuries are not a time of great events. The chroniclers recorded mainly trivia, like newspapers when Parliament is in recess. In 684 there was an earthquake in the Isle of Man. In 689 the rain turned to blood. In 691 the moon went red. The year 720 was the year of the hot summer. It is a salutary reminder that reality is not all composed of dramatic moments.

It is clear that around the middle of the eighth century this rare uneventful period came to an end. Bede himself is dead by then, so that we no longer have his help. The Welsh Annals and the Chronicle of the Princes go into less detail, and the Anglo-Saxon Chronicle is only slightly fuller. We must turn from the documents and instead look at the ground.

The extent of Mercia into what was previously North Wales is marked there in two phases. We may see that circumstances were evidently such that it was felt desirable to wall it off. The first great linear embankment, known as Wat's Dyke, is conjecturally dated to the reign of Aethelbald in Mercia, which ended in 757.

He is the last king to be mentioned by Bede, who says he came to power in 716 and ruled the whole of Saxon Britain south of the Humber. If he built Wat's Dyke it must have been an admission that he could not also rule Wales.

Wat's Dyke (now little more than the occasional bank or rise in the level of a field) runs in a straight northerly line from a point just north of Breidden, where the Severn curves, through Oswestry and past Wrexham to Hope, where it loops westwards towards Northop – indicating, interestingly, that Mercia had already by then overrun the coastal plain flanking the Dee estuary. The name comes from a figure of folktale in the area of Schleswig-Holstein from which this royal house of Mercia originated.

That Wat's Dyke is earlier than Offa's is probable both from the superior construction of the latter and from its more western siting. Mercia was undoubtedly expanding into North Wales.

Offa was the son of Aethelbald, and came of a distinguished line. Penda's dynasty had died out in 716, and leadership of Mercia fell into the capable hands of a noble family which had previously been in exile. Offa himself could look back to a famous predecessor, Offa I, in their home country, who had the distinction of being mentioned in a poem which is still extant, in which the kingdom he ruled is called Angel. Thus Offa of Mercia could read about his illustrious ancestor who ruled the country from which his people took their name, a hundred years before his time.

> . . . Offa, first of men, while still a youth, gained the greatest of kingdoms; no one of the same age achieved greater deeds of valour in battle: with his single sword he fixed the boundary against the Myrgings at Fifedor.

It is sometimes speculated that it is this mention of the setting of a boundary as being his ancestor's great achievement that gave Offa of Mercia his ambition. The feature he is known for now is undoubtedly a boundary line.

Offa's Dyke is indeed an ambitious affair. It runs in all for 150 miles from the South Wales coast to a point near Holywell on the north coast, and for some eighty of these miles it may be clearly seen today. In our present area it may best be seen near Chirk, where its bank-and-ditch form of construction are still quite apparent.

It is thought that this formidable earthwork would have taken a long period to complete, and its development must have occupied much of Offa's time during his reign and much of his available workforce. It would require a settled period, as work would have been impossible on such a scale under attack. A Welsh assault was significantly repulsed in

784, after which there was peace for a time, and it is likely that this date gave both the incentive and the opportunity for the start of construction.

Offa's Dyke was first studied in detail by Cyril Fox in the late 1920's, and has been the subject of equally painstaking investigation since. Noting its style of route-planning and its repeated responses to problems, Fox concluded that it was 'the product of one mind and the work of one generation of men'. The dyke uses westward-facing slopes, and it has its ditch (from which the bank was drawn) on the west side, clearly indicating that the builders were resident behind it to the east and that its purpose was to confront a westward-lying opponent. In its long course Offa's Dyke had many problems of terrain to deal with, and the ingenuity with which it kept to a direct route and almost a straight line is quite remarkable.

Offa's Dyke had its historical precedents. In its function of walling off a potentially troublesome nation which its builder had not the facilities to deal with, it was the direct equivalent of Hadrian's Wall. Offa's Dyke, in fact, is a thoroughly Roman construction, both in its political attitudes and its physical form, a determinedly straight line the only European equivalents of which, up to that date, are the great Roman roads. It is a manifestation of determination, clear-sighted policy, and power.

It is, however, a mistake to see the dyke, as Fox does, as representing the defence of civilisation against 'the wild highlander of the Welsh border'. The kings of Gwynedd and Powys had been well established, by the 780's, for more than two hundred years. North Wales' kings were Romanised, Christian and cultured, and the arts flourished at their courts – indeed some of the greatest Welsh poetry had already been written. Until the middle of the previous century the Mercians had been heathen savages, and at the date of the building of the dyke there is much more evidence for their military imperialism than there is for their art. The complete lack of documentation emerging from Mercia during the whole of the period suggests that the Mercians were not literate.

Since this is too long an embankment to have been militarily defended, it is interesting to wonder what it was for.

> And then Offa had a dyke made as a limit between him and Wales, so that it might be easier for him to resist the attack of his enemies, and that was called Offa's Dyke from that day to this.

So writes the chronicler in *Brenhinoedd y Saesson*, 'The Kings of the Saxons', the Welsh equivalent of the Anglo-Saxon Chronicle. This is a valuable reference, since the latter does not mention it at all. The idea of a limit, a boundary wall, is a credible one, and implies some sort of agreement. The agreement was likely to be stronger on Offa's side, however, since the dyke implicitly lays claim to the rich arable lands on its east for Mercia, and relegates the harder rocky uplands to its west to Wales.

It is interesting, from our present point of view, that it was evidently Offa himself who was still not satisfied with this. He wanted more. He wanted the continuation of the plain which runs along the north coast of North Wales, along the Dee, in its stretch beyond the dyke's end at Holywell, now the Prestatyn and Rhyl area.

This, at any rate, seems likely to be the area referred to as Morfa Rhuddlan, where a battle took place in 796. Offa was evidently there himself, since the great king died at Rhuddlan that year, still defending his newly claimed territory. This was the furthest that English lands had encroached into the North Wales heartland since the time of Edwin, and it was to be the furthest for some time to come.

The Welsh did not accept this extension lightly. The north-eastern plain is easily overrun, and guerrilla tactics in the hills were more suited to the local knowledge of the inhabitants than open pitched battles on the plain. Nevertheless Offa's son and successor Cenwulf was defeated and killed at Basingwerk, near Holywell, in 821, still having to fight for the extension of Mercia westwards. From that date on Mercia was heavily involved in a struggle for survival against a newly-powerful Wessex, which had risen to supremacy in the rest of the island while Offa and his heirs had been busy with Wales. The defeat of Cenwulf threw things into further disarray, and with an entirely new power-structure building up in Britain the great days of Mercia were over.

During all this time North Wales (or rather the kingdom of Gwynedd, since Powys had still not made its recovery to an independent status) had rather surprisingly been governed by a succession of undistinguished kings. Who has heard of Idwal Yrth, of Rhodri Molwynog, who died in 754, or Cynan Tindaethwy, who was succeeded by his son-in-law in 817? The last of these, however, became the grandfather of a king we have heard of, Rhodri Mawr.

There were battles during this period, of which we also know little, beyond the mention of them by the chroniclers. A battle between the Britons and the Saxons in 760, in Hereford, where the Britons lost a leader. 'Saxons', we are told, invaded the mountains of Snowdonia in 816. There was a battle at Llanfaes in 817, no doubt part of the inherited ambitions to extend Mercia. Clearly an expanding agrarian population had led to the need for new arable land, hence the interest in Rhuddlan and Anglesey, at a time when expansion the other way was curtailed by the rise and spread of Wessex. In the 840's and 850's the incidence of battles increased.

During this period we occasionally hear mention of Deganwy, so that presumably the ancient seat of the kings of Gwynedd was still defended. There was, as we shall shortly see, a need for a western frontier again. In 812 Deganwy was burnt down by lightning, so that the structure there must have been made of wood. In 823 it was burnt not by natural forces but by 'the Saxons' (*gan y Saesson*), who went on to overrun the kingdom of Powys, which they annexed. This would have been a raid by Ceolwulf, who succeeded Cenwulf in 821 as king of Mercia, making a last misguided attempt to extend westwards, while Wessex threatened him from the south and east. The Welsh chronicles use the term 'Saxons' indiscriminately to refer to the general groups of foreigners.

Egbert brought Wessex to dominance at this time, and according to the Anglo-Saxon Chronicle (though the Welsh ones do not mention it) he led his troops (real Saxons this time) into North Wales in 830. He reduced the inhabitants, the possibly biased chronicle asserts, to humble obedience. Perhaps some sort of peace was negotiated. Egbert, after all, could do with North Wales' assistance against any possible resistance movement in Mercia, which, from 828, he had amalgamated with Wessex.

Powys in the meantime had been overrun by the Mercians just in time for Mercia itself, along with Powys, to get absorbed into Wessex. The royal house founded by Cynan did however survive, though for much of the time powerless. This is significant because the heir of the line from Maelgwn (through his mother Esyllt), Merfyn, nicknamed Frych, the freckled, who became king of Gwynedd in 825, married Nest, the heiress of the house of Powys. Thus were united the two kingdoms which might otherwise have been in rivalry within North Wales.

The son of this union, Rhodri, became king of Gwynedd in 844 and when his uncle Cyngen died he became king of Powys too, in 855. He married Angharad, the daughter of a king of South Wales, and so also inherited territory further south when his brother-in-law, Gwgon, king of Seisyllwg (which is now part of Dyfed and West Glamorgan) died in 871. Thus for a time Rhodri, later titled 'the Great', ruled over more of Wales than any king before him and than most Welsh rulers after him. He also formed the base of the future lineage of Welsh princes, since to be descended from him was to be descended from all the rightful lines of Welsh royalty.

Although we have less details of the society of this time than we should wish, no-one should think of life in North Wales during the 9th century as being in any way backward or primitive. Both Merfyn Frych, who became king of Gwynedd in 825, and his son Rhodri, who succeeded him in 844, ran highly cultured and civilised courts. During their reigns in North Wales the seeds of Welsh literature were sown. It was during this period too that history started to be written, and the Welsh Annals were compiled in the form in which we have them now. The poetic cycle associated with the names Llywarch Hen, Taliesin and Aneirin, though the works of poets mainly connected with the north of Britain (and with references at least to a much earlier period) were largely a product of this age, and its flowering among Rhodri's allies is a reflection on the culture of his time. At the courts of Merfyn and Rhodri the art of writing was valued, and there the written records of Britain's history, traditions and poetic art were made which form the roots of the works we use today.

Rhodri found himself defending Wales from a new source of danger. According to the Welsh annals the first of the Northmen, as they were known, arrived in southern Ireland in 796. They began attacking the coasts of Britain soon after. In the early ninth century they had formed colonies on Wales' neighbouring seabords, on the islands of Scotland and in Dublin, and subsequently the Isle of Man. At the same time they put pressure on the eastern coasts of England. But it was seaborne raids from across the Irish Sea which formed the main problem for Rhodri.

The name 'Viking' is something of a nickname for these raiders, also known to the Anglo-Saxons as 'the heathen men' and to the Welsh as 'the Gentiles' (*Kenedloed*) or the Black Gentiles, *Kenedloed Duon*, in latin 'gentilium'. Sometimes the Welsh annals locate them more precisely as 'Normanyeit', Northmen, from which we can see the early formation of a word for future enemies, the Normans. The word 'Viking' comes from the Scandinavian word 'Vik', meaning a creek or bay, 'inga' meaning, as in Anglo-Saxon, 'person of', hence a coastal raider. The word is cognate with 'wicing', the word used by the Anglo-Saxons to describe pirates. As heathens the Vikings had no qualms about attacking monastic settlements, and became a great problem to these isolated and defenceless communities from their initial attack on Lindisfarne, in 793, onwards.

Their raids were felt at the time all over Europe. It is thought that they were caused by a number of political and demographic factors, mainly by a population explosion in terrain limited in cultivatable land. They came from southern and western Norway, and a separate group (politically better organised, and in fact destined to form a royal line of England) came from Denmark. The Danes had more effect on southern England than on Wales, and when we talk of Norsemen in the present context we should be thinking of Norwegians.

Rhodri won a major victory over them in 856 (at the very start of his reign) in Anglesey, which had been suffering the worst of their attacks, and by doing so he relieved not only his own people but neighbouring countries too. The Anglo-Saxon Chronicle speaks in chorus with the Welsh Annals when it records the onslaughts of the 'heathen men'. They ravaged Sheppey in 835. They formed a settlement there in 855. They occupied Thanet, the homeland of the first settlers, in 865. Meanwhile the Welsh annals say that while some leaders died in battle with the Saxons others were killed by the 'black heathens', and in 853 the black heathens had overrun and laid waste Anglesey.

Rhodri had the unenviable task of fighting two determined enemies on two different fronts. His victory against the Northmen brought him no peace. He was at once engaged in war with the West Saxons, this time in protection of his inherited kingdom of Powys. That, as we have seen, had fallen to Mercia in 822, thus becoming a Wessex claim in 828. Evidently however the people of Powys had not entirely given up hope of retaining some of their land, and the fight went on.

It as to be Rhodri's personal undoing, and he and his son fell in a battle against the Mercians in 878. He was succeeded by his son Anarawd, and there is evidence that his people did not forgive his enemies his death. When Anarawd defeated a troop of Mercians on the river Conwy in 880 the battle was known as *Dial Rhodri*, Rhodri's revenge. At this time another curious twist to North Wales' political history took place, when the kingdoms of North Wales became allies of the Danish Vikings established at York, presumably because both were at that time implacable enemies of the Mercians. The reason for the presence of Mercians on the Conwy may be due to pressure from the Danes, the Mercians being once again in need of fertile land into which they could expand, since by 877 the whole of Mercia east of Watling Street had become part of the Danish kingdoms. Their previous king, Ceolwulf, had retained western Mercia only by co-operating with the Vikings, and indeed he had Danish help in his attack on Gwynedd in 877, when a battle in Anglesey known as 'the Sunday battle' forced Rhodri into brief exile in Ireland, from where he returned the next year to confront Ceolwulf again, and to be slain.

> Eight hundred and eighty was the year of Christ when the battle of the Conwy, which was called 'the avenging of Rhodri', took place.

The battle was later said by Camden, in the 16th century, to have taken place on the spit known as Cymryd, opposite Glan Conwy, a little up the river from Conwy. Anarawd sent the invaders back to Mercia, and for a time we hear no more of them.

This is not the case, however, with the Northmen. They overran much of South Wales at this time, and parts of England; but North Wales was not neglected.

> Eight hundred and ninety was the year of Christ when the Black Norsemen (*y Nordmannieit Duon*) came to Gwynedd.

In spite of all this attention the Northmen formed no permanent settlement in North Wales. Rather surprisingly, in view of this, their most durable remains in North Wales are various place-names around the coast. 'Anglesey', for instance, is a Viking name: it means 'the island of the strait', 'Onguls-ey', and its lesser offshoot, now commonly known as Puffin Island, was termed by the Norsemen 'Preistholm', from the fact of its already well-established monastery ('Holme' being the old Norse word for 'island') which is the formal name which it still bears. Other Viking names surviving in this area are those of a point near Beaumaris, 'Osmund's Eyre' (commonly known now as Gallows Point) and the Skerries (from 'sker', meaning 'reef'), a group of rocky islets which are Anglesey's further extension into the Irish Sea. Moreover it is likely that the name of that massive limestone headland, the Orme, is of Scandinavian source, being derived from the Old Norse word 'warm', meaning serpent and hence sea-monster, from which we also get the word 'worm'. The name Worm's Head, on the Gower peninsula in South Wales, a similar outthrusting snake's head of land, almost certainly comes from the same Viking origin.

Apart from these place-names the Vikings left very little evidence of their presence in North Wales. They formed no settlements and deposited very few artefacts. A Viking grave was found near the seashore near Prestatyn in the 1930's, and a few silver and bronze ornaments in Anglesey. Coins from the later period of Viking settlement in Dublin were found on the Great Orme at Llandudno at 1980, suggesting possible trading after the decline of hostilities.

During the 890's the Danish settlers in Britain (as opposed to the Norwegian colonists raiding the Irish Sea shores) became an organised alliance, and swept across the country in a form known to the Anglo-Saxon Chronicle as 'the force'. They reached the old Roman town of Chester in 893, and barricaded themselves in the remains of the fortress there, where they were besieged by King Alfred's army of West Saxons. These set about depriving the Danes of their supplies by destroying the crops in the old roman 'prata' of the Cheshire plain, and commandeering their cattle, so that the next year they were forced to leave their refuge. They responded to this crisis by mounting a raiding expedition into North Wales, in 894, but we did not have to entertain them for long. Having helped themselves they set off east again, and North Wales' brief encounter with the Danelaw ended the same year.

Sea-borne raids from Dublin however continued, and twice in the next century (in 961 and 971) the monasteries of both Holyhead and Penmon were attacked. The royal seat of the kings of Gwynedd at Aberffraw was itself destroyed by Viking raiders in 968. On our other border there was less conflict, since Mercia was by now thoroughly subordinated to Wessex. There remained the residue of resistance in Mercia, and in 923-4 the North Welsh found themselves again in alliance with Mercia against Wessex, when a revolt blew up centred on Chester, causing the Wessex king, now Edward 'the Elder', to march north to subdue it.

As the millennium drew to a close the long-drawn-out dissension between Gwynedd and its neighbours came to a weary conclusion. In 943 the ancient kingdom effectly ceased, for the time being, to exist, when Edward's son Edmund of Wessex defeated and killed King Idwal of Gwynedd, and placed the whole of Wales in the hands of his ally Hywel Dda, king of Dyfed in South Wales. Wessex itself was not to survive much longer either, and in the early years of the new era, in November of 1016, a later Edmund was obliged to partition his kingdom and share it with the Danish king, Cnut, who thus became the king of Mercia.

Bibliography

Ancient Monuments Commission Inventory: 'Anglesey'. HMSO.
A History of Wales. John Davies. Allen Lane.
Anglo-Saxon Poetry selected and trs. R.K. Gordon. Everyman.
Pre-Conquest Cheshire. J.D. Bu'lock. Cheshire Community Council.
Brut y Tywysogion (Peniarth Version, and Red Book of Hergest Version, 2 vols.) and *Brenhinoedd y Saesson*. trs. Thomas Jones, University of Wales Press.
A History of the English Church and People. Bede. trs. Leo Sherley-Price. Penguin.
Celt and Saxon. Peter Berresford Ellis. Constable.
'Dykes, Cyril Fox. *Antiquity* vol. III No. 10, June 1929, p.135.

TABLE ALLIES AND ENEMIES OF NORTH WALES, 7th to 9th centuries

Date	Event	Alliance	Opponent	
604	Aethelfrith unites Deira and Bernicia; Edwin exiled to Gwynedd	Gwynedd & Deira	Bernicia	NORTHUMBRIA ASCENDANT
613	Aethelfrith invades Gwynedd.			
617	Battle of Chester	Deira, Mercia, Gwynedd & Powys.	Northumbria	
	Edwin regains power.	Gwynedd v. Mercia v.	Northumbria	
633	Edwin killed by Cadwallon & Penda.	Gwynedd & Mercia	Northumbria	MERCIA ASCENDANT
642	Death of Oswald	Gwynedd, Powys & Mercia	Northumbria	
675	Peace brokered by Theodore	Gwynedd, Mercia & Northumbria	Wessex	
757	Offa becomes king of Mercia	Gwynedd v. Mercia v.	Wessex	
825	Merfyn becomes king of Gwynedd	Gwynedd & Powys	Wessex	WESSEX ASCENDANT
844	Rhodri becomes king of Gwynedd	Gwynedd, Powys & South Wales	Wessex & Vikings	
877	Rhodri exiled	Mercia & Danes	Wales	
893	Revolt in Chester	Wales & Mercia	Wessex	

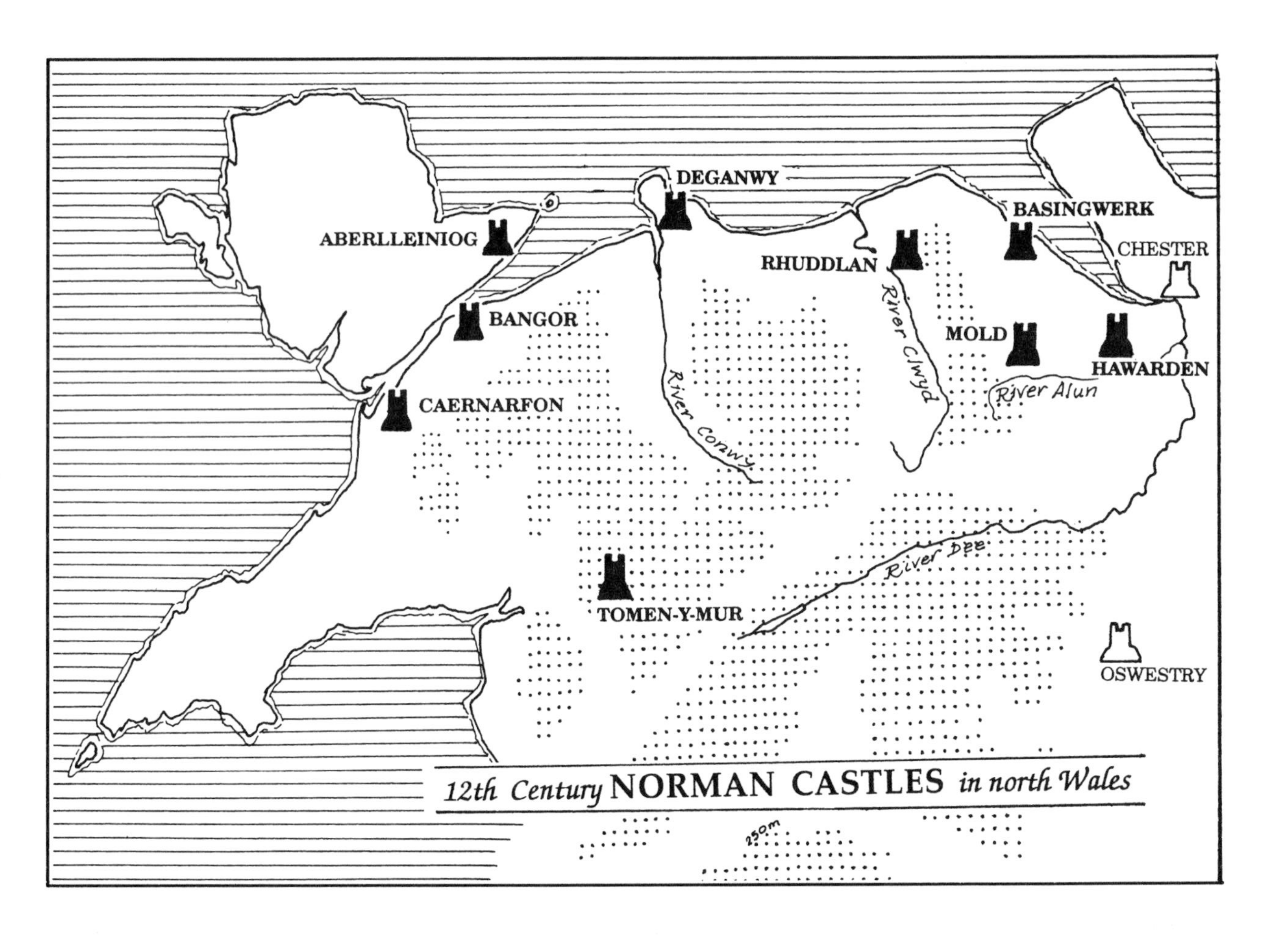

DEGANWY
ABERLLEINIOG
BASINGWERK
CHESTER
RHUDDLAN
BANGOR
MOLD
HAWARDEN
River Clwyd
River Alun
CAERNARFON
River Conwy
River Dee
TOMEN-Y-MUR
OSWESTRY
12th Century NORMAN CASTLES in north Wales
250m

Kings, Lords and Princes

At the time when Anarawd, the son and avenger of Rhodri Mawr, was ruling over Gwynedd, a company of Norwegians, under their leader Rollo, won from the western Frankish king an area of northern France. It started with a patch of the lower Seine valley, in 911, and was extended by agreement westwards to incorporate the province of Rouen and the channel shores. From the start the Franks recognised it as a duchy, and Rollo was the first Duke.

This was a long way from Wales, and for some time remained remote, but with hindsight (always a useful tool for historians) we cannot help feeling that the two forces had within them from this time, like the iceberg and the Titanic, the destiny which was eventually to bring them into fatal collision.

Normandy, as it then became, was politically organised from the start, and no mere fiefdom of the Franks. Sufficient proof of this is that by 1066 Rollo's descendant, William, found himself powerful enough to invade and occupy the realm of England.

How and why this took place need not concern us here. What is significant for North Wales, in the immediate case, is that it gave rise to a new political form on our border. In the long term it was to prove more radically influential, since this was not the end of the Norman expansion and like a relentlessly spreading tide it lapped forwards for centuries across Europe, until it eventually enveloped North Wales.

The immediate effect of the Norman occupation of England was a new form of government. Strictly speaking it was not exactly new: nothing in history ever is. It was the form which expanding empires had consistently used before, familiar to us in our particular case as that used by the Romans to protect Britannia against the Picts.

The principle is that a king cannot be in two places at the same time. Thus if he is king of both England and Normandy he can shuttle backwards and forwards between the two but in each case will be presenting his departing back to the other. He thus needs a friend to stay behind.

The Romans used the system of client kingdoms or buffer states to watch their backs, those groupings who had recognised the benefits of the *pax Romana* and were willing to pay a bit in terms of independence for the sake of not having to contest the might of Rome. The bargain is fairly even-handed. Loyalty is bought by a guarantee of rights over territory and of a certain amount of power. Loyalty is the hostage with which a powerful lord can negotiate with a king. It is necessary to bear this in mind in order to understand such people as Hugh d'Avranches, first earl of Chester, and Roger of Montgomery, his counterpart at Shrewsbury.

Feudalism was not an innovation of the Normans, but it came to them from their Frankish neighbours and, having some flair for political development, they put it to good use. It was new in Britain when they brought it here, or rather its Roman form had long fallen out of use. Later the term came to apply mainly to an agricultural system, but in its origins it was military.

Originating in France at the end of the Roman occupation, it was developed by Charlemagne as a social and land-owning system during the eighth century. The original principle was that someone of lower status could enjoy the protection of someone more powerful in reward for providing the latter with support in war when needed. This hierarchy was of a pyramidal form, working tier by tier from the local lord of the manor and his villeins through the lords, barons and earls, and ending in the lonely pinnacle of the king.

The system adapted well to the use of 'marcher' lords to protect the kingdom's borders. The effects on North Wales were both immediate and permanent, and they took effect from the first years of the Norman Conquest. It was William's policy to appoint the strongest of his trusted associates to the most vulnerable places, and once there, of course, they set about trying to improve their personal position. Thus it was that the earls of Chester and of Shrewsbury were not content with occupying one side of the (by now more or less established) border of Wales. They wanted to occupy as much as they could of the other side of it too.

To understand what the position was in Wales at the time it is necessary to go back to the death of Rhodri Mawr, in 878. His extensive, even unwieldly, kingdom was divided between his sons, which was the normal Welsh custom. Anarawd, as we have seen, became king of Gwynedd and Powys. From his line are descended the later rulers, Owain Gwynedd and the two Llywelyns. Cadell ruled the territories further south, though Rhodri had never been king of the small kingdom of Dyfed. Cadell's son, Hywel Dda, married into the royal family of the latter, and on the death of his father-in-law, its king, in 904, he became king of Dyfed.

On the death of his relatives of the house of Gwynedd, and with

English support, Hywel became king of all Wales, and his descendant Gruffudd ap Llywelyn, who reigned immediately before the Norman Conquest, in fact ruled over more of what is now Wales that anyone else before or after.

Gruffudd ap Llywelyn was a determined, ruthless and ambitious man. Although many of his activities took place in South Wales and its English borders, and so cannot concern us here, it was under his rule and through his militancy that some of the Cheshire and Shropshire borderland was regained for Wales, in the 1050's, four hundred years after Powys had first suffered reduction on the invasion of the Northumbrians and three hundred years after Mercia had expanded into Cheshire from the line of Wat's dyke to that of Offa's.

These acts of Gruffudd's are of importance to us because, although they were soon reversed, they lay in the background of the border situation when the Marcher Lords arrived, after the Conquest. They had symbolic force, representing Welsh ambition and English resistance, and combined with the ambitions of the Norman lords themselves they spelt a future of conflict and dispute.

Gruffudd was defeated by Harold of Wessex in 1063, forced to flee into the mountains of Snowdonia, where he died on 5th August. According to the Welsh chronicles he was killed by his own men, an outcome which may be explained by his habit of killing all who opposed him, which doubtless left many deep scars and hunger for vengeance over the course of his long reign.

After the defeat and death of Gruffudd ap Llywelyn in 1063 Wales became disunited again, and in the years immediately after the Conquest Gwynedd and Powys were separately, and not notably strongly, ruled by the late king's half-brothers. Indeed the years immediately after the Conquest saw a state approaching civil war in Wales, with the sons of rival factions fighting each other, a chaotic situation from which Bleddyn, the king of Gwynedd, emerged temporarily victorious, in 1069. Bleddyn himself however was killed by treachery in 1075, and it was not until the emergence of Gruffudd ap Cynan as king of Gwynedd in 1081 that anything like order became apparent.

William the Conqueror's initial intention had been to leave the Welsh borders alone, but a rebellion shortly after the Conquest by the earl of Mercia, Edwin, in collaboration with the Welsh, quickly changed his mind. Edwin was removed, and Roger de Montgomery (who took his name from his home town in Normandy and only later gave it to his new home on the Welsh border) put in his place.

William himself had come to Chester in 1069, and the first castle there was a royal stronghold. In 1077 however he handed it over to Hugh of Avranches, nicknamed Hugh the Fat, like Roger a frontiersman by background, whose home of Avranches lies on the coast and on the border of Normandy with Brittany. William's placing of these two forceful potentates on North Wales' border is a recognition of his need for their help there, and the considerable freedom which he allowed them to use in harrying the Welsh gave to their two houses a status, and an independence, which he and his successors were to come to regret.

William's chief worry was a coalition of Welsh and Mercians, which had become a possibility while Edwin ruled Mercia and Bleddyn Gwynedd. The installation of the two ambitious lords was intended to prevent this, and he did the same in mid Wales by giving territory to William Fitsobern. In due course his son William Rufus followed this practice by installing a relative, Roger of Poitou, at Lancaster, in 1092, to act as a buffer between the Welsh and the Scots.

For a time this worked well enough, at least from the Norman point of view. The rights of the rulers of South Wales were recognised, in exchange for payment of a fee. Hugh of Avranches however was less accommodating, and for much of the rest of the 11th century the earldom of Chester extended well into North Wales.

Hence it is that major Norman fortifications occur well within Wales. Roger, Earl of Shrewsbury, built himself a castle at Montgomery, which he named then after his Norman home town. Hugh of Chester ruled as far west as Rhuddlan, where he established a stronghold and placed in charge of it his cousin Robert. Most castles before 1100 were wooden structures secured by earthen banks, and only in the second decade of the next century did the Normans start building those great stone constructions which we associate with them today.

Along with the main centres of the earls a spate of lesser castles dotting our countryside testifies to the activities of their henchmen and supporters. The system, filtering downwards, spread unendingly. The king was supported by the earls, but the earls in their turn needed the support of their knights. Each knight was allocated a patch of land, in return for his military service. They cannot all have built themselves castles to govern these, but even those which remain in Wales and its borderland, which presumably were seats or campaigning camps of lesser lords and of the earls themselves, number at least five hundred, and in our area there is a concentration of them towards Shrewsbury.

The 'motte-and-bailey' castle is a simple and highly functional affair. The motte part was a mound thrown up in the middle, from which it was possible to look out at the surrounding countryside over the top of the stockade, the bailey, which was the second ingredient of the castle's form. On top of the mound (which wherever possible made use of a natural hill) was a wooden tower, in which the lord and his retainers would stay. The foot soldiers and the knights' horses would be housed in the bailey below.

There are so many of them in some areas that it seems likely that they were not all in use at once, but rather thrown up in the course of a campaign as conditions required. Surprisingly, perhaps, for artefacts which have endured so well, a motte-and-bailey castle is a quick and easy thing to construct, so that we do not need to think in terms of any elaborate planning or long-term aims. Depending on the number of people available a period of a few weeks, perhaps eight to twelve, would be sufficient, so that these may be seen as little more than temporary camps.

The form was in use for a considerable period, from the early years of the Conquest up to the period of permanent construction in stone of regional centres in the 13th century. Examples of the remaining mottes, or 'tumps', can be seen in many parts of North Wales, both towards the border, as along the A5 in the Dee valley near Llangollen, and well into Gwynedd, as at Bala and Tomen y Mur.

Such tumps along the border are explicable, representing the incursions into Wales of the Earls of Chester and their henchmen. More surprising are the ones which occur far west into Gwynedd, for instance at Aber, where a tumulus is still clearly visible near the stream. At Bala the Tomen was at one time a focal point of the town, now, enclosed by housing and planted with shrubs, much less conspicuous than in its heyday. Like the mound at Tomen y Mur (which is close to a Roman camp) it was in antiquity thought to be Roman, but that is largely because everything old was assumed to be that; in fact it is now recognisable (as is Tomen y Mur) as the motte part of a motte-and-bailey, and so allocatable to a broad 11th-12th century date, and to a style introduced by the Norman lords. A striking mound above the west bank of the River Conwy at Tal-y-cafn, of which nothing is known, was also traditionally associated with the Roman camp at Caerhun, but is also clearly of the later period and style. It served to protect this ancient crossing-place of the river, but for whom and under what circumstances?

More surprising still is the realisation that Caernarfon castle itself is based on a Norman motte, demonstrating a Norman presence in the heartland of North Wales long before Edward I. In fact the castle here is recorded twice in the 12th century, once when Giraldus Cambrensis came through with Archbishop Baldwin in 1188, when he says that Caernarfon is so called because it is 'the castle of Arvon'. In the same century the biographer of Gruffudd ap Cynan records the castles built by Hugh, Earl of Chester in the reign of William Rufus, and mentions the one at Caernarfon as being in the old Roman city. The mound of it was largely removed during the last century, but its incorporation into the structure of Edward's castle has affected the way the latter was built, and the eastern end (particularly as seen from the quay) reveals evidence in its sloping masonry of this use of the former fortress.

Similarly at Rhuddlan Edward used the motte built by Hugh's cousin Robert, so that we know there was a fortress there from the end of the 11th century. Thus it is that from border to coast the Marcher Lords had prepared the chain of refuges which were eventually to lead to the completion of the invasion.

There were to be many setbacks in the course of this progression, and they started almost at once with the accession of William Rufus. In 1093 an uprising in South Wales was quelled, but resistance by the Welsh was not the king's only problem. In 1088 Roger de Montgomery led his private army, including a Welsh element, into the Midlands in an attempt to take Worcester. The attempt failed, but this did not stop his son and successor, Robert, launching an attack against Henry I in 1102, for which he forfeited his lands and was sent home to Normandy. Similarly Hugh II of Chester lost his earldom after taking part in an unsuccessful rebellion against Henry, in 1173-4. Once again we see the complexity of the situation, and the difficulty of determining who was on which side and fighting against whom.

In the meantime the North Wales Welsh had been taking advantage of the king's troubles. When William II went to Normandy to protect the interests of his brother Robert, its ruler at the time, who had gone on a Crusade, they took the opportunity to destroy the Norman castles in Gwynedd. A few years later the Normans took revenge, sending an army under the Earl of Shrewsbury as far west as Anglesey. The men of Gwynedd took to the hills and sought help from Ireland. There followed some confusion when a seaborne raiding party of Germans arrived at the same time, and the chroniclers almost give up in the face of explaining the alignments of Welsh, Irish, Normans and Germans. We are on much surer ground by 1098, since it was in that year that Gruffudd ap Cynan returned from exile in Ireland.

Gruffudd's father had fled to Dublin in 1039 when the kingdom which should have become his was seized by his relative, Gruffudd ap Llywelyn, who, as we have seen, was ruthless and ambitious and spared no-one who opposed him. Doubtless it was prudent of Cynan to emigrate. The effect of this could not have been foreseen, but it was crucial for

North Wales. It brought about the end of Viking hostilities, and hence enabled a period of stability and expansion in North Wales which had not been possible for several hundred years.

We have to remember that Dublin was at this time a Viking city. It had become a settled colony as early as the end of the eighth century, and it was to remain in Viking hands until its seizure by the Normans in 1170. The ability of the ousted kings of North Wales to take refuge there means that the relationship of North Wales to the Norsemen was at least negotiable. When Cynan went there it was definitely with peaceful intentions.

Cynan in fact went further than that; he married a local girl, with the result that his son, Gruffudd, king of Gwynedd, was half Norse. When he came back to North Wales in 1081 it was with a rabble of Viking mercenaries.

The chronicles say that he made peace with the French (that is, the Normans), and that he received Anglesey. In fact his territory is likely to have extended further than this, and his biographer, writing in Latin within two decades of his death, makes it clear that he was the king of inner Gwynedd, the heartland which ran southward to the Mawddach and east as far as the Conwy. From that base he eventually expanded into Powys and towards the Cheshire border, and by his death in 1137 he ruled over much of Mid Wales as well.

The Normans had undoubtedly had aspirations in North Wales, which Gruffudd was responsible for curtailing. In 1090 they had pushed as far as Anglesey, where Hugh of Avranches, Earl of Chester, built himself a castle. This, near the coast of Penmon at a spot called Aber Lleiniog, may still be seen in the form of a substantial mound, though the masonry ruins which now surmount it are a part of a later castle than Hugh's, which was made of wood. In 1094 this fell to the Welsh under Gruffudd, and its taking was a main factor in the Norman abandonment of North Wales during the next hundred years. It was, it seems to have been decided, not worth the effort.

From the security of his power-base Gruffudd did much to restore the prestige and dominance of the ancient dynasty of Gwynedd, lost to the line of Hywel Dda a hundred years before, and threatened with extinction by his descendant Gruffudd ap Llywelyn. His was another age of art and culture. Not least among his achievements was his facilitating the reign of his son, Owain Gwynedd, who inherited a peaceful and prosperous kingdom when Gruffudd died, in 1137, at the great age of 82.

To understand the lineage of the Welsh princes one has to envisage two lines, both emanating from the marriage of Rhodri Mawr (whose parents' marriage had made him the heir of both Gwynedd and Powys). One line falls through Owain Gwynedd to Llywelyn the Great, to end in Llywelyn the Last. The other descends through Hywel Dda and the lords of South Wales to culminate in the House of Tudor. To complicate this simple pattern a link between the two occurred through the Mortimer family, when Roger Mortimer, whose mother was the daughter of Llywelyn Fawr, married a descendant of Gruffudd ap Llywelyn; from that union eventually came the English House of York, so that both sides at the Battle of Bosworth could claim descent from Rhodri Mawr and his ancient forebears of the throne of Gwynedd.

Owain Gwynedd's reign has left us with visible proof of its stability. It is to this period, the second half of the 12th century, that many of our early stone-built churches belong. It is a certain sign of a settled age when people have sufficient confidence in the future to build in stone.

This was the time of the construction of great monastic buildings as at Penmon in Anglesey where the Priory Church dates largely from Owain's time. The fine Norman arch in the church of Aberffraw also dates from this reign, as do parts of the much simpler upland church at Llanrhychwyn, above the Conwy valley. Several of the older churches of the Lleyn peninsula have stonework belonging to their origins at this date, and the elegant church of St Beuno at Pistyll, which conveys its age largely through its beautiful simplicity, has remained largely intact in its 12th century form.

By the time of the reign of Owain the Welsh themselves had started to build castles, adopting the Norman style of motte-and-bailey. It is thus quite possible that some early castles attributed to the Normans were in fact built by the Welsh, though in many cases documentary evidence tells us which was which. There is no doubt for instance that the great earthen embankments and central mound of Tomen y Rhodwydd, between Ruthin and Wrexham, near Llandegla, south of Llanarmon, was built by Owain himself. It is referred to in the 'Brut' entry for the year 1148, with the words 'Owain ap Gruffudd ap Cynan built a castle in Ial'. It lies at the border of Gwynedd and Powys and near to the boundaries of them both with the earldom of Chester, at the head of the winding Nant y Garmon defile which runs up from the Vale of Clwyd to the slight plateau on which it stands. It is no coincidence that this major fortification lies in an area which had by then become traditionally a claim of the earldom of Chester, and its presence here is a statement of defiance at this critical time in the balance between North Wales' independence and the Norman advance.

Tomen y Rhodwydd is an earthwork, rather than a castle in the later sense, as its mound was topped by a wooden structure. It is known that that castle did not survive for long, since it was burnt by a rival Welsh chieftain in 1157, in the aftermath of Henry II's invasion and the brief chaos in the area which resulted in Owain's coming to terms with the English king and the latter's return to England. This is at any rate the way the sequence reads in the entry in the 'Brut'.

Owain's earthwork, with its firmly rounded mound and its deep steep-sided moat, has a curiously intimate, personal feel about it. It is quite clearly a classic example of the motte-and-bailey form, a borrowing from his nation's Norman enemies, yet retaining the emphasis on high embankments reinforced by deep ditches which are such a strong feature of ancient Welsh hillforts. Indeed the only points of difference between the fort of Owain's and those of his ancestors a thousand years before, is that his is smaller and low-lying. The pace of technology of course took much longer than a thousand years to start speeding up, and old forms were an adequate response to old problems.

A deep moat surrounds the high mound, and continues in a long loop around the bailey, where the steep outer slope of the bank displays a formidable obstacle to assault. The mound is 24 feet high and 66 feet across, and the whole complex fills about an acre. It had one entrance, which may be seen on the north side.

It is important to remember that Owain Gwynedd was a king, restoring to the ancient kingdom founded by Maelgwn a good deal of the prestige and power it had in the meantime lost to the Saxons of Wessex. Towards the end of his reign he occasionally used the term 'Princeps' instead of 'rex', but this was not for him a diminution of power. Rather he saw himself as king of Gwynedd and prince of a much greater stretch of Wales. The latter title eventually became recognised by the kings of England, and as the immediate descendants of Owain came to think of themselves as rulers of an amalgamated country the term 'king' fell into disuse.

Things had been happening in England which help to explain how Gruffudd and Owain had the breathing space in which to establish their power. In fact there was confusion from the start in the matter of inheritance of the throne. William the Conqueror's eldest son, Robert, was designated future Duke of Normandy by his father before his death, and the throne of England was bequeathed to his second son, William Rufus. When the latter died, in a hunting accident which may have been not so accidental, in the year 1100, unmourned by his family, his nation and by history, he was succeeded by his only slightly less unpopular brother, Henry I.

North Wales in the meantime had not been quite neglected. William II had brought a force into Gwynedd, but was defeated and sent home. Henry I moved with a much more intimidating force in 1114. No less than three armies converged: from Chester along the coast, from the southern Welsh border, and across the Berwyns in between. They converged at Tomen y Mur, as had the main Roman roads. What the early Norman kings demanded chiefly was homage and tribute. Gruffudd ap Cynan paid up, and as a result was thereafter left in peace. This was greatly to the advantage of the house of Gwynedd, and while the English throne continued on its problematic course Gruffudd ap Cynan quietly consolidated his kingdom and gradually extended its boundaries unhampered.

On Henry's death there was again no clear line of succession, and the throne of England was for a time disputed, indeed divided, between two of William I's grandchildren, Mathilda, Henry I's daughter, and Stephen of Blois, son of Henry's sister.

Mathilda had been married by her father to the Count of Anjou, Geoffrey Plantagenet, in the hopes of ending territorial rivalry over the Norman lands of the kings of England. This hope proved vain, and Henry died, in 1135, while fighting his son-in-law in Normandy. Although her marriage was at the time a disadvantage to her inheritance, it was to prove of the utmost long-term significance. Britain has never known, and most probably never will, a rule as powerful and long-lived as that of the Plantagenets.

How it came about that the son of Mathilda and Geoffrey of Anjou came to be King of England need not concern us here. The fact that he did, however, had great repercussions in North Wales. After the havoc of the reign of Stephen England was thankful for a strong king, and Henry Plantagenet, now Henry II, enjoyed sufficient security to turn his attention to his borders.

North Wales was at the time divided, once again. The ruler of Powys sought the new king's help in defending his kingdom against the incursions of Gwynedd, and Henry expected, and got, his help in return. When he came into Wales to display his power in 1157 he did so with Madog of Powys' support.

The king pressed on into North Wales and clashed with Owain at a battle at Basingwerk, near Holywell, an area where the kings of Gwynedd had confronted their invaders several times before. There a pitched battle took place, in which Owain's forces gave the king's a severe battering. At the same time the forces both of King Henry and of Madog of Powys were pillaging Anglesey, and Owain could not contain his enemies on two fronts. Henry, meanwhile, gathered his troops and brought them along the shore from Chester to Rhuddlan, which had temporarily fallen into Owain's hands. 'And then peace was made between the king and Owain.' We do not know a lot about the terms of this peace, but it had the result of Owain being allowed to continue to rule over Gwynedd, and of the king going home.

It seems clear that one reason for the mutual eagerness for peace was that the campaign had gone badly for both sides. Henry, though great in power of arms, and supported by a fleet from South Wales, nearly came to grief in a wood near Basingwerk, where he might well have lost his life. In the attack on Anglesey the combined English and Powys force was ignominiously routed by the locals, and the king's son slain. It was largely as a result of this event that Henry was willing to come to terms with Owain. Owain meanwhile had found himself overstretched at Rhuddlan, while events in Anglesey were taking place out of his reach. It cannot have appealed to either side to go through all this again.

One of the conditions was that Owain should stay within the traditional border of Wales, giving England the land between Chester and Rhuddlan, much disputed over the centuries. It was Owain's encroachment into this that had caused the arrival of the English king.

We also know that the peace between the two countries did not endure. Owain was still both an able and an ambitious man. A resurgence of Welsh pride during the 1160's focussed on Owain as its figure-head.

To a large extent the Welsh were now taking advantage of the difficult position the king of England had put himself into by his quarrel with Thomas à Becket. There is no doubt that Owain Gwynedd was an astute politician as well as a strong campaigner, and such a man could spot a fatal weakness in his enemy. The trouble which Henry had brought about with the Becket case threatened his throne and kept his attention focussed close at hand. Owain took this chance to regain much former Welsh territory.

Although the king was otherwise occupied, he could not afford to let things go too far on the North Wales border. It is significant that without direct help from the central monarchy the earls were not powerful enough to withstand Owain's advances. Owain had already recaptured Rhuddlan and extended his rule as far as the Dee. The land between the rivers Dee and Clwyd, a fertile and relatively flat part of North Wales, is known as Tegeingl. English people inhabited it, in 1165. Their forced removal and the theft of their goods and cattle formed the trigger which had the king hurrying north. He clearly feared the escalation of this incident into an invasion of Chester itself.

> And when the king of England thought that there was fighting against his castles which were there, he moved a host with great haste and came to Rhuddlan, and he camped there three nights. And he returned again to England and gathered a host beyond number of the picked warriors of England and Normandy and Flanders and Gascony and Anjou and all the North and Scotland.

So the Peniarth version of the 'Chronicles of the Princes' informs us. Clearly Henry meant business.

First he went with this massive force as far as Oswestry, 'thinking to annihilate all Welshmen'. Instead, he found all Welshmen ranged against him. Along with Owain and his brother Cadwaladr and their force from Gwynedd were the armies of Powys and South Wales. These encamped together near Corwen. There for a time the two vast armies stayed, neither willing to make the first move.

It was Henry eventually who became impatient. He moved his forces into the Ceiriog valley, where he had the woodland felled to facilitate their movement. He had chosen his ground unwisely, since the Welsh could confine him to the valley, and fight there on their own terms. Henry, realising this after an initial skirmish, in which losses were about equal, moved upwards onto the slopes of the Berwyn mountains. 'And he stayed there a few days.' Yet even this was a mistake. He had reckoned without the Welsh weather.

> And then there came upon them a mighty tempest of wind and bad weather and rains, and lack of food; and then he moved his tents into England.

One sympathises. Influenced, perhaps, by this harsh introduction to the pleasures of North Wales, Henry did not try invading again. Instead he turned to more diplomatic measures, and appointed his opponent in South Wales, Rhys ap Gruffudd, his Justice, with power over much of Wales. Although in theory this did not extend to the north, Rhys' position of deputy to the English king made him, at that time, the most powerful man in Wales.

This could only have come about, in 1172, in the aftermath of the death of Owain Gwynedd. When Owain died in 1170 (the same year as the murder of Thomas à Becket) he left the succession undecided. His heir apparent was his eldest son, Iorwerth. There seems, however, to have been conflict and competition between Owain's sons, and the leading contestant to emerge from this was Dafydd, a son by his second wife, who eventually took the kingdom of Gwynedd by force rather than by right.

> The following year Dafydd ab Owain gained possession of all Gwynedd after having expelled from it all his brothers and all his uncles.

Dafydd moreover consolidated his position by forming ties with the English monarchy. He married a half-sister of the king, Emma, who was an illegitimate daughter of Geoffrey of Anjou, in 1174.

Dafydd's succession to the kingdom (now more usually known as the principality) of North Wales left a problem for the future, and this in turn exacerbated North Wales' weakness in the face of an increasingly powerful Plantagenet monarchy on its border. Again and again it is remarked that if only North Wales had been unified it could have been strong. The annals for the last years of the twelfth century teem with quarrels amongst relatives.

Powys had also split in two, and under the leader of the one part of it, Gwenwynwyn, an uprising took place in the year 1198 which for a brief time seemed capable of uniting the people of Wales against the enemy, still referred to as 'y Saeson', in spite of now being very far removed from their Saxon predecessors. Gwenwynwyn's effort failed, and with it his position of leadership. In the meantime a new leader had emerged, who was to put the principality of Gwynedd back in its ancient position of dominance over Wales.

Llywelyn was the son of Iorwerth, the eldest son of Owain Gwynedd, whose inheritance had been passed over in favour of his half-brother Dafydd, largely through the latter's ruthlessness. Llywelyn was only twenty-two when he seized much of the princedom from his uncle, in 1194. He did not gain complete control of Gwynedd until the death of his cousin Gruffudd in 1200 and dispossession of his other cousin Maredudd ('because of his treachery') which followed it in 1201. These were the sons of Cynan, son of Owain Gwynedd, with whom he had co-operated to remove their uncle Dafydd. These lords ruled areas of Gwynedd for a time, and it is thought that the castles of Garn Fadryn, inside the extensive hill-fort on the Lleyn peninsula, and Aber Iâ near Porthmadog, where there is still a motte indicating a castle of the Norman style, were fortresses of these local rulers.

The family in-fighting might well have gone on for several more generations had it not been for Llywelyn's personal ability and instinct for diplomacy.

In the year 1199 Richard the Lionheart (who had reigned for ten years) was succeeded by his brother John as King of England. King John was in a weak position through most of his reign, as his capitulation to the barons in the signing of Magna Carta illustrates, but he had an unusual degree of knowledge of Wales, being, before his accession, himself a Marcher Lord. The feature which had mainly marked the reign of Richard I was his absence; he left at once for the Holy Land and spent much of his reign on crusade. With John the situation was different. Although he had substantial problems with his continental territories, he spent a good deal of his time at home.

By the time John gained the throne Llywelyn ap Iorwerth had established himself as ruler of most of North Wales. John's first instinct was to use against him the old principle of divide and rule. He attempted to use the lord of Powys, Gwenwynwyn, as a counter-force. He shortly realised that it was too late to weaken Llywelyn by such means, and, himself not short of cunning, decided that friendly relations were the safest, on this inconvenient border of his empire, and with this powerful but diplomatic prince.

Llywelyn had much to gain from compliance, and the price of it was no more than an oath of loyalty. In 1201 he accordingly swore it, and in return was allowed to keep unmolested the territory he had so far won. A few years later, in 1205, the alliance was sealed in what had by now become the traditional way: Llywelyn wed the English king's illegitimate daughter, Princess Joan. With things now apparently stable and amicable, it is surprising to find the two leaders so soon embroiled in war.

To begin with certainly things went well. Llywelyn was allowed to occupy Powys, which John had annexed after trouble from Gwenwynwyn, and in 1208 he thus extended his principality to the whole of North Wales. In 1209 he joined the English king in a war against the Scots.

Historians have struggled to identify what it was that then went wrong, but the most likely explanation was that King John was of highly unstable temper. In 1211 an army gathered at Chester. It consisted not only of the royal force of England, but contained too the men of several Welsh leaders, the dispossessed local chieftains of North Wales and the exiled princes of Powys, a package of envy and revenge which marked the end of Llywelyn's ascent.

The earls of Chester had not ceased to be involved in border quarrels which evidently stretched well into Gwynedd. So useful to them had become the fortress at Deganwy, mentioned by Giraldus in 1188, that Llywelyn himself had destroyed it. In 1210 however the Earl of Chester, then Randle Blondevil, rebuilt it, prompting Llywelyn to raid the earl's lands around Chester in retaliation. It was in the immediate aftermath of these events that King John's army mustered.

Llywelyn's response to the gathering of the considerable army was the time-honoured Welsh one. He evacuated the borderland and took refuge in the mountains across the Conwy, where he could wait. They took their cattle and supplies with them, leaving the border country and Anglesey empty.

Thus the king came unobstructed to Deganwy. The vast army camped there on the Vardre, but without supplies. Llywelyn had apparently retained the ability to prevent access overland from Chester, and it seems the English had brought no fleet with them. With the country in between empty of cattle they stayed at Deganwy until they starved, unable to make the next step of crossing the Conwy river into the land held by the Welsh.

> And there the host suffered lack of food to such an extent that an egg was sold for a penny-halfpenny; and they found the flesh of their horses as good as the best dishes.

So the *Brut y Tywysogion*, 'The Chronicle of the Princes', tells us. About Whit Sunday the king gave up, having lost many of his men, and 'returned in shame to England'.

Yet he was clearly a stubborn and determined man, and it was as soon as August that he tried again. He came this time with an army even bigger and fiercer, marching up from Oswestry this time, and so perhaps approaching the barrier of the Conwy river at a higher point. This time, at any rate, he crossed. He built castles as he went, we are told, presumably of the temporary motte-and-bailey form, since we cannot identify them. A wing of the army went ahead to Bangor, which they burnt. Llywelyn was not supported by his neighbouring and subordinate lords, and his advisers pressed him to make peace.

This he did in the same year through the emissary of his wife, the king's daughter. Llywelyn had to pay, to be precise to the amount of twenty thousand cattle and forty horses; he had to pay too in the loss of land, of that long-disputed stretch of fertile ground between the Conwy and the Dee, known as the Perfeddwlad. This was too much for him to tolerate in the long term, and it must have been an expedient to get the army out of Wales.

If the Welsh leaders thought that by reconciling themselves to the English king they could regain a degree of independence they soon found they were mistaken. By the end of the year King John was having a castle built at Aberystwyth, which the princes who had so recently been fighting with him to reduce the power of Llywelyn recognised as a sign of his intentions. They burnt it down. By 1212 Llywelyn found that he could lead a grand alliance of the Welsh against the English.

They besieged all the king's castles in Gwynedd, and took them all except Rhuddlan and Deganwy. These, it is clear, were solid stone-built structures, whereas the others may well have been wooden campaigning forts more vulnerable to siege and destruction. The king at any rate regained these important sites. When in 1213 he gave territory to Owain, the son of Dafydd, whom Llywelyn had exiled when he took control of Gwynedd, he specifically excepted the castle of Deganwy. In 1214 however even this fell to Llywelyn, along with all the castles of the Perfeddwlad.

Llywelyn in the meantime had built castles of his own. Whereas the castles of his grandfather Owain were earthworks topped by timber towers, Llywelyn himself built in stone. Castell y Bere is one such, perched on a crag overlooking the Dysynni valley between Barmouth and Tywyn, an important location at the southern end of his princedom. It was built in 1221 in the course of a quarrel with his son Gruffudd, from whom Llywelyn had taken the area of Meirionnydd which Gruffudd had been ruling. Another castle thought to have been built by Llywelyn is Castell Carndochan, above Bala lake.

Far away on the other edge of Gwynedd Llywelyn very probably built Ewloe, where the imposing ruins are now largely hidden in a wood. This may however have been one of his grandfather Owain's foundations, like Tomen y Rhodwydd, later developed and used by Llywelyn as a base for his challenge to King John. The castles far into the heartland of Gwynedd must represent, on the other hand, his need to keep in check his rival local lords. Ewloe's present tree-crowded seclusion gives it a misleadingly peaceful air, and it takes an effort of imagination to appreciate it as part of a warlike struggle.

Llywelyn did not neglect the defensive site favoured by his ancient ancestors at Deganwy, when the earls of Chester were not occupying it, and some traces of the ruins excavated there belong to his period. The main remains however are a little later, and we shall be hearing of its continuing use.

One other place of key importance strategically is Dolwyddelan, since it controls the north-south line of communication, the route by which one could reach (as the Romans did) the uplands around Trawsfynydd and thence the road southwards. Dolwyddelan castle stands on a natural prominence above the Lledr valley, almost Disneylike in its romantic perfection.

There is a tradition that Dolwyddelan was built in 1170 by Llywelyn's father Iorwerth, and indeed there was a motte castle nearby before the present stone one. That may have been the site of the second part of this tradition, that Dolwyddelan was Llywelyn's birthplace. This is often assumed to have been the present fine tower, but that was almost certainly first built by him and extended by his grandson and by much later additions still. Dolwyddelan as it stand today is in fact something of a romantic revival – the battlements, for instance, were added in 1870. The original keep was only two storeys high.

These early Welsh stone castles were all rectangular in shape, whereas at this time the more easily defended round tower was gaining favour amongst the Norman Marcher Lords. When Llywelyn came to build Dolbadarn, in about 1230, he introduced the fashionable innovation of roundness. He had been working towards this break-through for some time, as is indicated by the D-shaped towers of Ewloe, Castell y Bere, and Cricieth, which he also built in about 1230.

Dolbadarn, like Dolwyddelan, controls a route through the hills, in fact the Llanberis pass. The siting of Llywelyn's castles seems to have had stategic, rather than administrative, purpose. Throughout this period the centre of his court's activities, in the governing of his considerable realm, was the llys, or 'court'.

It is interesting that Llywelyn's courts do not seem to have been major fortifications. They were the administrative centres of a country secure enough to have civil rather than military buildings. The castles were for defence, and these have survived. We know that both existed at the same time, and no doubt the castles facilitated the royal progress from court to court. Like all medieval rulers Llywelyn had to keep on the move, to show his presence in different parts of his principality on a more or less continuous basis. We know the sites of his courts, but cannot trace them on the ground today. There was one at Trefriw in the Conwy valley, traditionally said to be where the Village Hall now stands. The present parish church at Trefriw was said to have been originally founded by Llywelyn, to save his wife the Princess Joan the steep walk up the hill to the older, already existing, upland church of Llanrhychwyn. The location of the important court at Aber is a matter which is disputed but not yet proved. The undoubtedly ancient house called Pen y Bryn stands on a hill which shows clear signs of fortification and is a firm contender for the site, and not far away a rival site is provided by the medieval motte alongside the stream. At Beddgelert (where the later story of the faithful hound perhaps commemorates a genuine connection of the town with the great prince) a house called Llywelyn's Cottage, by the bridge, may possibly be the site of the llys. In two places the centre of the commote (the administrative area) did coincide with the area's castle. Both of them, interestingly, are coastal. Llywelyn had a court at Deganwy, and at Cricieth.

Llywelyn built Cricieth castle, and moved his local court to there, in the 1230's. The castle as it now stands, however, was to a much greater extent the work of his grandson, also Llywelyn, and of their enemy and final conqueror Edward I, and as such we shall mention it again.

One of the most important of Llywelyn's courts, and the one to have best survived, was that at Conwy. Here we have the remains now of the only stone-built domestic building of Llywelyn's reign. The great hall of the court, now known as Tŵr Llywelyn, was incorporated into the town walls of the garrison town by Edward I. As a result we have the anomaly now of a row of windows in a town wall, surely yet another feature in which Conwy is unique.

Llywelyn evidently spent much time at Conwy, and it was there that he chose to be buried. The reason for his affection for the place is his particular interest in the abbey, to which he gave its first charter, in 1198. It was not new then, since Giraldus had noted its existence in 1188. In fact it was probably founded in 1186, when the 'Brut' notes that a community of monks came from Strata Florida into Gwynedd. There is no doubt that princely patronage led to its expansion and rise in status, so that it became one of the most prominent abbeys in Wales.

Aberconwy Abbey was a Cistercian house. The Cistercians had been in Wales for more than forty years by then, based on their monastery at Whitland, near St Clears in South Wales. Conwy was their first outpost in North Wales, itself an offshoot of the Cistercian colony at Strata Florida in Mid Wales. They favoured isolated sites with no existing settlement, where they could live their simple life-style and provide for themselves, largely pastorally, on previously unworked land. A further group founded an abbey at Cymer, near Dolgellau, also the site of one of Llywelyn's castles.

Another monastery in which Llywelyn took a personal interest was that at Llanfaes, near Beaumaris in Anglesey, which lay opposite his coastal seat at Aber and could be reached from there across the Lafan sands by road and a short ferry crossing. This was a Franciscan house, founded by Llywelyn to be a burial place for his wife, the Princess Joan, who died in 1237. Although nothing remains to be seen of it today, a flourishing port and a sizeable town developed at Llanfaes during the 1250's, in time to be removed wholesale by Edward I when he built Beaumaris nearby. Recent excavation has revealed the foundations of large stone buildings and a surrounding wall, which may have formed one of Llywelyn's courts. Crockery of the 13th century ties them to this period.

One last sad vestige of the great monastic centre and community at

Llanfaes remains in Beaumaris church. There rests the coffin of the Princess, wife of the great Llywelyn and daughter of the King of England.

> Notum sit omnibus sanctae matris ecclesiae filiis, tam presentibus, quam futuris, quod ego Lewelinus Gervasii filius totius Northwalliae Princeps . . .

I, Lewelinus, son of Gervase, prince of all North Wales. Clearly Llywelyn was adjusted to his position, as a feudal magnate licensed by the Angevin king to hold, untramelled, a client kingdom. Playing by the rules, he was allowed to wield very considerable power, and the building of fine stone castles argues a high degree of prosperity, as does the sponsoring of noble abbeys an equivalent amount of civilisation. The increasing complexity of the world he lived in meant that he had to be more than a feudal baron; he had to be a diplomat as well, and in this he comes across to us as something of a modern man, prepared to use the conventions of his enemies and also to exploit the weaknesses of his compatriots, in the course of fulfilling what we would like to think were patriotic as well as personal ambitions.

Llywelyn both built and destroyed the castle at Deganwy, which was traditionally a possession of the earls of Chester. He pulled it down for the second time in 1241, and for the second time the Normans rebuilt it. It was thus that when the King of England invaded Wales again, this time King John's son Henry III, in 1245, we again find an English army encamped at Deganwy.

Henry, now aged 34, was at the height of his power. There had been a delicately sustained peace between him and Llywelyn, who had gone through the correct procedure of doing him homage on his accession and had been confirmed as a reward in his possession of North Wales. But Llywelyn died in 1240, and rule over Gwynedd was inherited by his son Dafydd.

Dafydd was Llywelyn's chosen heir, his son by the Princess Joan, but a previous liaison had produced an elder son, Gruffudd. The accession of Dafydd was supported by Henry, who was after all his uncle. All seemed likely to go well, as might be expected with this level of support. At a treaty signed near St Asaph in 1241 Dafydd agreed to part with some of his lands, including Deganwy, as part of Gruffudd's inheritance which would be held for him by the Crown. To ensure this, and as a sort of hostage for Dafydd's compliance, Henry took control over Gruffudd himself, whom he imprisoned in the Tower of London. This subtle arrangement was spoilt by the unfortunate Gruffudd, who died while trying to escape, in March 1244. He had made an improvised rope out of sheets, and it broke.

It was the convenient removal of this possible rival which emboldened Dafydd to provoke the English king. With considerable Welsh support on his side he broke the St Asaph treaty and reclaimed his territory.

Henry came with his army, as others had before and would again, to Rhuddlan, thence to Deganwy. There he confronted the fortress of the Snowdonia mountains, where Dafydd remained secure. Matthew Paris, the contemporary chronicler, quotes at length a letter from a soldier with the army on the Vardre, writing in that September to a friend in England, from which we get an unusually explicit first-hand view of the Conwy river, in the autumn of 1245:

> There is a small arm of the sea, which ebbs and flows under the aforesaid castle (where we are staying), and forming a sort of harbour, into which, during our stay here, ships have often come from Ireland, and from Chester, bringing provisions. This arm of the sea lies between us and Snowdon, where the Welsh quarter themselves, and is, at high tide, about a crossbow-shot wide.

He further records how a raiding party sacrilegiously plundered the Abbey of Aberconwy, on the Welsh bank, for which they received the well-deserved reward of being hanged and dismembered by the furious Welsh. Some, the writer tells us, preferred to risk drowning and

> threw themselves of their own accord into the waves, there to perish.

The same fate befell Henry as had overtaken his father; his army was inadequately supported by sea, and although ships bearing provisions from Ireland (which he was also invading) came into the river, one such went aground on the further bank and fell into the hands of the Welsh.

> There was no wine in the king's house, and indeed, not amongst the whole army, except one cask only; a measure of corn cost twenty shillings, a pasture ox three or four marks, and a hen was sold for eightpence. Men and horses consequently pined away, and numbers perished from want.

Ignominiously, like his father, Henry retreated, leaving many corpses unburied. He managed however to retain possession of Deganwy castle, and in fact issued a charter to the borough there in 1252. Dafydd had in the meantime died, and was succeeded by his elder brother Gruffudd's second son, another Llywelyn, who had campaigned with him in the recent wars. Llywelyn ap Gruffudd for a time ruled jointly with his brother Owain, and being under severe pressure the two brothers made peace with the king of England, at Woodstock, in April 1247. The terms were that they were to renounce their rights to the Perfeddwlad, the land between Chester and the river Conwy.

Henry thus had a large swathe of the best land in North Wales in the personal possession of the Crown, no longer letting it to a Marcher Lord. He had in the meantime commandeered the earldom itself, when Earl John died childless in 1237. Trouble in his continental realms called him away from the Welsh border, in the 1250's, and he left the rule of England to his son Edward, granting him the annexed earldom and the Perfeddwlad.

> The following year Edward, son of King Henry, earl of Chester, came to survey his castles and his lands in Gwynedd.

It was thus that, in 1256, the future Edward I came to Deganwy, and looked across the Conwy river to the further hostile bank for the first time.

Bibliography

Welsh chronicles, as previous chapter.
A History of Wales, John Davies. Allen Lane.
Castles of the Princes of Gwynedd. Richard Avent. HMSO
Dolwyddelan and Dolbadarn Castle. Richard Avent. Cadw.
Oxford History of England: 'Domesday Book to Magna Carta'. A.L. Poole; 'The Thirteenth Century'. Sir Maurice Powicke. Oxford, Clarendon.

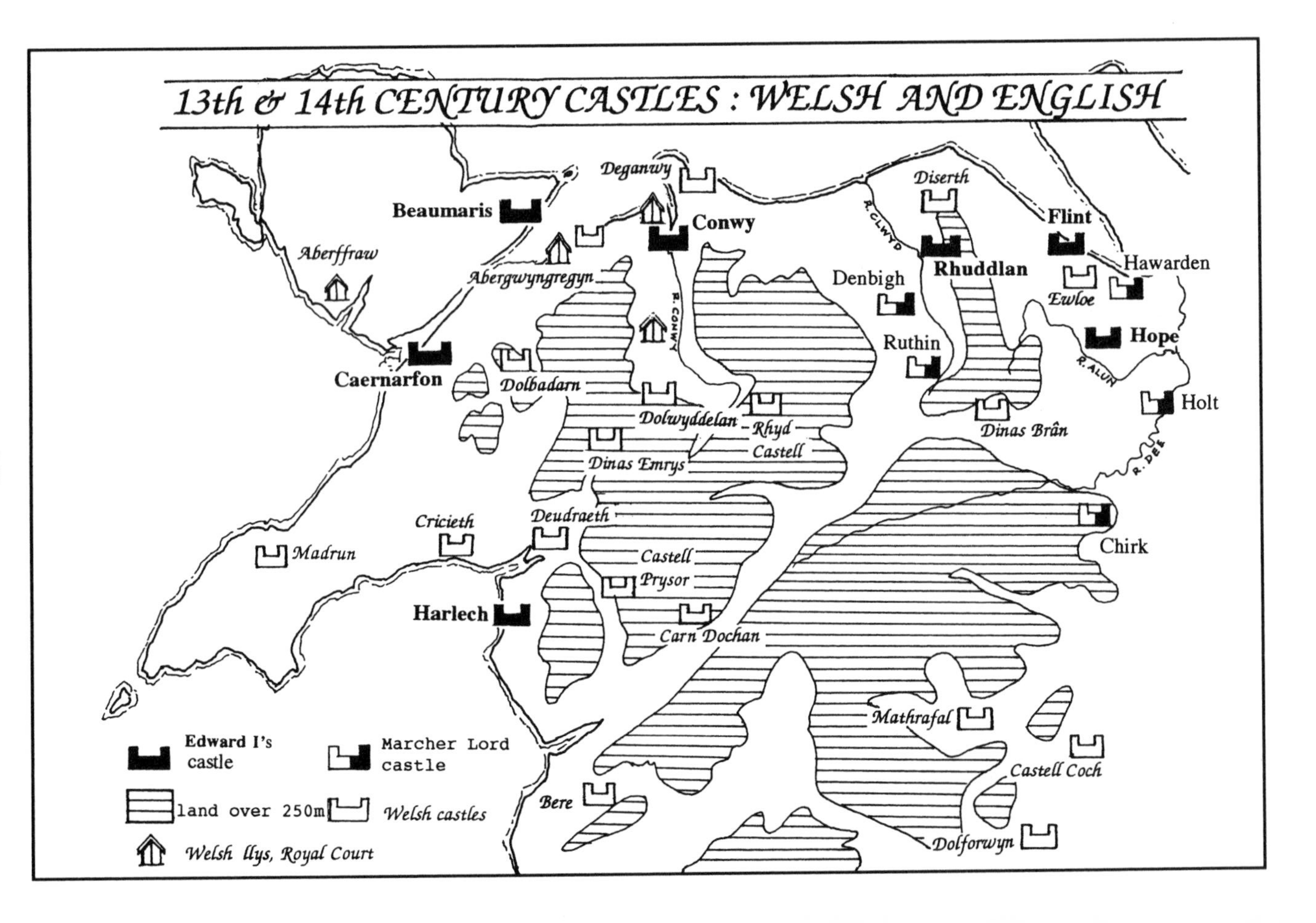
13th & 14th CENTURY CASTLES : WELSH AND ENGLISH
Deganwy
Beaumaris
Conwy
Diserth
Flint
Hawarden
Aberffraw
Abergwyngregyn
R. CLWYD
Denbigh
Rhuddlan
Ewloe
Hope
R. CONWY
Ruthin
Caernarfon
Dolbadarn
R. ALUN
Holt
Dolwyddelan
Rhyd Castell
Dinas Brân
Dinas Emrys
R. DEE
Cricieth
Deudraeth
Chirk
Madrun
Castell Prysor
Harlech
Carn Dochan
Mathrafal
Castell Coch
Bere
Dolforwyn
Edward I's castle
Marcher Lord castle
land over 250m
Welsh castles
Welsh llys, Royal Court

Llywelyn and Edward

At the beginning of the 1250's Llywelyn seemed to be in an impossible position, only nominally a prince of North Wales (his power confined to that of a vassal lord, in part of inner Gwynedd) and beset by the powerful forces of the English king. By 1257 he had reversed this balance, and in 1258 he announced himself to be Prince of Wales (and not just Gwynedd) and posed a definite threat to his powerful neighbour, the Lord Edward.

Llywelyn ap Gruffudd often seems to us a tragic figure, burdened in history with his epithet, 'the Last', weakened by a running quarrel with his brother Dafydd, and by the latter's treachery, and famous mainly for his fateful death. In fact it is apparent from events and from the attitude of contemporary chroniclers that he was a capable, strong-willed and intelligent leader, much loved by his countrymen.

Edward, given a free hand by his father, had gone too far, too soon. He had imposed on Wales at this early stage of its subjugation the sort of iron rule for which he would in due course become justifiably famous. He had done so without taking account of the resilience of his victims. The Welsh leaders were still proud men; they had not yet been deprived of that quality.

> And then the magnates of Wales, despoiled of their liberty and reduced to bondage, came to Llywelyn ap Gruffudd and mournfully made known to him that they preferred to be slain in battle for their liberty than to suffer themselves to be trampled upon in bondage by men alien to them. And Llywelyn was moved at their tears.

Knowing now that he had this support, he acted fast. Within a week (in 1256) he had thrown out Edward's henchmen from all his castles in the Perfeddwlad; he moved on into Meirionnydd and Ceredigion, and ousted Edward there. He put men loyal to himself and to Wales in the areas he conquered, and removed from all parts of Wales those Welsh leaders who had sided with the English. He made a policy of giving the conquered lands to his supporters, 'keeping naught for himself, but only fame and honour'.

It was thus that in March 1258 he obtained an oath of allegiance from all the Welsh princes, and himself adopted the title Prince of Wales.

It was in this role that he could negotiate from a strong position with the English barons, and King Henry realised that Llywelyn posed a serious threat. He brought an army to Deganwy in 1258, stayed there the month of August to September, and went fruitlessly back to England. Deganwy castle, which Llywelyn had not yet managed to control, was in a state of siege from 1257 until it finally fell in 1263. In 1259 there was a shaky truce, against the wishes of some of Llywelyn's enemies amongst the barons.

In 1263 and 1264 the King of England and his son and heir had considerable problems with their own barons, amounting effectively to civil war. 'That year the Welsh lived in peace with the English, with Llywelyn ap Gruffudd prince over all Wales'. This peace did not however prevent Llywelyn from finally taking Deganwy castle, and, like his predecessors, destroying it – this time for ever.

During his reign Llywelyn had added substantially to his grandfather's castles, consolidating his (for a time) considerable power. He added a surrounding wall and the western tower to Ewloe, when he took it back from the Lord Edward in 1256. He probably built a second tower at Dolwyddelan, which he made something of a headquarters. He added the outer ward to Cricieth castle, making it a substantial fortress, and he changed the entrances here, so that the castle is approached now from (as it were) behind, giving even less chance of storming its inner gateway. More rashly, he built a castle of his own on the very edge of his possible territory, in the Marcher country of the Severn valley, at Dolforwyn, almost nothing of which now remains. It was one of the first casualties of the outbreak of war, in 1276. Dinas Brân, above Llangollen, had in the meantime been built by Llywelyn's supporter, the lord of Powys Fadog, in the 1260's, although it was fated to become a Marcher castle during the forthcoming war. It occupies the site of many previous fortifications, going back to Iron Age times. Indeed it is such a naturally fortifiable place that it is only remarkable that it ever fell out of use, as it did when its Norman owner, John de Warrenne, who gained possession of it and the surrounding territory as the spoils of war in 1282, transferred his attention to his new castle at Holt.

Llywelyn's power was such that it could not easily have been destroyed from outside. Instead his weakness lay within his country, and indeed his family. His rise to power had not been unopposed, and he had dealt with the competition in the same way as several of his ancestors. In 1255 he met his two brothers Owain and Dafydd in battle, and defeated them. Owain he then kept in prison from that year until 1277, when he was forced to release him as part of the terms of the Treaty of Montgomery. It was said by Leland in the 16th century that Owain suffered his long imprisonment in Dolbadarn castle, which seems quite likely to be true.

Dafydd was also initially imprisoned by his masterful brother, but (evidently seeming less dangerous than Owain) he had been released before the Treaty and for a time sided with the king, in England, against his barons. He too was restored to his possessions in Gwynedd by the Treaty of Montgomery, and in his case this was to prove fatal for the independence of Wales.

North Wales' destiny did not in the end rest on any matters of military or economic power, but on the characters of three people, Llywelyn, Dafydd and Edward, and on a number of largely chance events.

Although Dafydd is normally portrayed as being treacherous and sly, his position can be partly understood if it is borne in mind that the inheritance system in Wales has never been based on primogeniture; indeed it can be seen today that the custom of division of possessions between all the children had led over the centuries to the proliferation of small-holdings and the consequent veining of our hillsides with boundary walls. On the several occasions when North Wales had been ruled by one powerful leader, the element of force which was necessary to achieve this left always in the background the disaffected members of his own family. So it was with Dafydd. That the results were particularly unfortunate for Wales as a whole casts his deprived position in an unfavourable light.

In 1264 the government of England, and control over the king, had fallen into the hands of Simon de Montford. This situation was not to last long, but while it did Llywelyn came to terms with the new ruler. In 1265 de Montford, nominally on behalf of the king, recognised Llywelyn's position as Prince of Wales, but on the condition that he held it as a vassal of the king of England, and at the price of a fine of £20,000, payable over ten years. In the same year, however, a rebellion of barons led by Edward, who had escaped from de Montford's prison at Hereford, which was in effect an attempt to rescue the king from de Montford's power, put an end to the matter at the Battle of Evesham. Since both sides fought in the king's name it is hardly surprising that Henry was the victor, and it now behoved Llywelyn to clarify his position. His deal with de Montford had been guarded and qualified, and was clearly a safeguard against the latter's increased power. Now there was no doubt who was in control. Two years later, consequently, it was necessary for Llywelyn to renew his treaty, and incidentally pay another fine, this time of 25,000 marks.

The Treaty of Montgomery of 1267, which had been negotiated in advance by the papal legate, was surprisingly advantageous to Llywelyn. It officially confirmed the title 'Prince of Wales', giving him overlordship of all other Welsh rulers. It recognised his rule over the Perfeddwlad, the territory between the earldom of Chester and the river Conwy, which had previously been given to Edward. The only condition seems to have been, apart from the fine, that he do homage to the king as Prince of Wales.

Henry, after the recent upheavals and in a state of continuing unrest among the barons, needed the money, and even more he needed the resultant peace with Wales. Although it confirmed Llywelyn's rule over the territories he had seized, the Treaty also effectively drew a line around them. So far, but no further, was the essence of the arrangement made at Montgomery.

Much of Llywelyn's success in rising to be lord over a Wales returned to its traditional extent was gained at the expense of the Lord Edward. It was his lands, given him by his father, on the Cheshire border and in Mid and South Wales which Llywelyn had overrun. Thus when in 1272 the king died, and Edward, now aged 33, found himself (though away on crusade) king of England, there was a ready-made scenario for further trouble.

Edward did not come back from the Holy Land until 1274. In his absence he had demanded Llywelyn's homage, which had been refused. The Prince of Wales had increasingly, during Edward's absence, been retreating from the terms of the Treaty, delaying his annual payments and overstepping the agreed bounds of his principality by building Dolforwyn castle, near Montgomery.

1274 was a bad year for Llywelyn. Edward came home in August, and in the same month was crowned. Earlier that year Llywelyn's brother Dafydd, who had defected to England as long ago as 1262, and been restored to his lands in Wales as part of the arrangement made by the Treaty of Montgomery, conspired with the leader of southern Powys to oust Llywelyn and take over the principality. Llywelyn moved against the traitors at once, but they fled to England where they were given royal protection.

Under such circumstances Llywelyn could not be expected to do homage, to a king who was harbouring his enemies. It would have been directly against the feudal code, on which the agreement and indeed the very idea of 'homage' was based. A vassal leader is entitled to retain his lands for his own use on the condition of asserting loyalty; for that he gains protection from his enemies supplied by the greater power. The 'Brut' is quite clear about the reasons for Llywelyn's refusal, and in terms of the time they made good sense.

> In that year, about the last feast of Mary in September, king Edward came from London to Chester; and he summoned to him prince Llywelyn to do him homage. And the prince summoned to him in turn all the barons of Wales. And by common counsel he did not go to the king because the king harboured his fugitives, namely, Dafydd ap Gruffudd and Gruffudd ap Gwenwynwyn. And for that reason the king returned enraged (*yn llidyawc*) to England.

Angry, or enflamed. Edward was a man not used to being contradicted. His actions throughout his life show a strong element of autocratic willfulness. Yet he displayed a quite remarkable degree of patience, for someone so prone to anger, with Llywelyn. Indeed he sent for the prince three times more, and received only complaints. The last time, in April 1276, would have seemed to have been final, but even then Edward continued to attempt to negotiate. He sent the archdeacon of Canterbury to Wales as his emissary, and Llywelyn duly explained his terms. He would not risk going to London. It cannot have slipped his memory that his father, Gruffudd, ended his days in the Tower. He would do homage at Oswestry or Montgomery, but only after his wrongs had been put right. Edward, on his part, would consider no conditions. Llywelyn's submission had to be absolute.

Llywelyn was fully aware of the danger of the situation. He 'frequently sent messengers to the king's court to seek to arrange peace between them, but he did not succeed at all'. It cannot have helped matters that in 1275 Llywelyn, though now well into middle age, married for the first time; in what seemed to Edward to be an outright threat of insurrection he married the daughter of Simon de Montford, Edward's defeated enemy, who had been given sanctuary in France. They were married by proxy at an earlier date, but Edward reacted with surprising alarm at the possibility of the de Montford trouble being resurrected in Wales. Such a late and distant marriage does not seem likely to have been an action of the heart, and we may well suspect Llywelyn of political motive.

When the princess sailed to join her husband, in 1275, her ship was boarded in the Bristol Channel, and she was taken to Windsor, where she was detained. This act amounted to provocation, and made it conclusively impossible for Llywelyn to undertake the required homage.

A little less relentlessness of attitude on either side would have done the trick. But here we are not dealing with relenting men. Edward and Llywelyn faced each other with the obduracy which goes with strength.

Yet their position, at least in their own eyes, was more than reasonable. To Edward, Llywelyn had broken the Treaty of Montgomery by refusing to do him homage. To Llywelyn it was too high a risk for him to go to do homage at a court where his enemies were honoured guests.

It is of course impossible to view this disagreement dispassionately, knowing as we do its fatal outcome. Both parties had their justifications, particularly in feudal terms, and both were also wrong. Llywelyn was asking for a reasonable act of justice, which Edward was wrong to refuse. It Llywelyn was a legitimate prince, then Dafydd was a traitor. Yet Llywelyn was, as he must have known, on very weak ground. He was not even the eldest son, which was Owain, and in any case, as has been remarked, the Welsh did not recognise the right of primogeniture. By the laws of his own land his brother Dafydd was fully entitled to a share of the kingdom, which was what he had sought. It could thus be argued that what Llywelyn was demanding was not justice.

On 12th November 1276 Edward in full council declared Llywelyn 'a rebel and disturber of his peace'. This was a declaration of war. By January the war had begun. Edward started by fortifying his castles in the Marches, and Llywelyn found himself confronted across his whole border. Edward had quickly recovered the lands won from him, the Cheshire borderlands and the area around Montgomery. From the start he operated a policy of recruiting discontented Welsh support. In South and Mid Wales castle after castle which had been in Welsh hands was handed over with little resistance to the king, lord after lord promised him his support.

Edward himself came to Chester to deal directly with Llywelyn in June. What is most impressive about his particular way of treating things is the formidable order and organisation with which it was all arranged. Between January and June a plan which had been in preparation since the previous November was meticulously carried out, under the capable supervision of expert administrators and with the backing of trained and efficient troops. When he came to Chester Edward knew that a great part of his victory was already achieved. He had the border and a large extent of Wales already under control, and a vast mobile army at the ready to move on North Wales. In Chester he was supported by a fleet, which came into the Dee from the Irish Sea under the command of the Warden of the Cinque Ports. Moreover he had the support of a good part of the supposed enemy. When, in the summer, his army reached a total of 15,640 available men, some 9,000 of these were Welsh.

It is difficult to understand why the Welsh had in part turned against their great leader, but we cannot help noticing that they had done it before, and (when Owain Glyndŵr's rebellion lost its initial impulse) they were to do it again. If there is an innate distrust of central leadership in the Welsh temper, this might be aggravated by the dictatorial way such leadership was occasionally exercised. Behind such desertions seems to lie the feeling that it is preferable, because conducive to greater freedom, to be governed by an alien king at a distance than by a ruler of your own close by.

In June 1277 much of the western edge of the Cheshire plain was still covered by dense forest. Edward had woodmen and road makers in his army, just as he had every other conceivable sort of expert. A great swathe was cut through the forest so that the large army could advance.

Providing such a route from Chester into North Wales was essential to Edward's strategy. Chester could then supply his forces as they pressed further into the enemy country, both by land and by sea. Either Edward knew of the form of the Roman campaigns in North Wales, or alternatively he was simply a master-strategist in the Roman style and so chose the same solutions. We do not know which. We know that his methods coincided very precisely with theirs.

An invading force needs good lines of communication and safe refuges a day's journey apart, which are thus able to support each other and which, in this case, can alternatively be assisted by sea. To have a fleet based in Chester is essential to the conquest of North Wales. So is the building of a string of fortifications.

In July Edward started to build Flint castle, which was to be his headquarters in North Wales while work was taking place to expand the old Norman fortress at Rhuddlan. In August he was in Deganwy, where the castle was still unrepaired after Llywelyn's destruction of it, so that he and the army must have camped. It was then, in August 1277, that he took the fateful decision not to rebuild Deganwy, but to build instead, in the Roman manner, a fortress defending the far, not the near, side of the river crossing.

To take the west bank of the Conwy must have been Edward's ambition for some time, probably since he first looked across the river when he came as Earl of Chester. Without control of the western bank he could not command the river, and his supply ships, as he knew from his father's experience, entered it at risk. With a castle on the further bank he could not only dominate the land and sea routes, the harbour and the river crossing, but could strike from that base into the heartland of Snowdonia.

Several things had to take place before that was possible. In the meantime Edward's effective tactics continued to follow the Roman pattern by undermining North Wales' food supply. In August the grain crops of Anglesey, on which (now that the Cheshire plain was in Edward's hands) the principality relied for flour, were growing ripe. His fleet landed in Anglesey during the first two weeks of September, and the grain was harvested by three hundred and sixty reapers working for the English Crown.

This was a blow which Llywelyn could not sustain. He came to Edward at Rhuddlan and offered to submit, and a treaty was signed at the Abbey of Aberconwy, on 9th November, 1277.

This was a very different matter to that of Montgomery, and it smacks of the sad state of a defeated country. Nevertheless it was a treaty, and it brought peace. There is on the face of it no reason why Edward should have agreed to terms at all. He could simply have proceeded to occupy Wales, as indeed he eventually did. By November 1277 Flint and Rhuddlan castles were built and in use, and their existence suggests the forming of a plan to continue the chain of castles which eventually occurred.

But in 1277 Edward was evidently not ready to go on. It would have been considerably more difficult for him to campaign in the mountains of Snowdonia (which was virtually all that was left of independent Wales) during the winter months. The campaign had already been a long one, lasting (with its planning stage) a full year, and it must have been straining Edward's exchequer. We may read between the lines of the Treaty of Aberconwy the need for a pause for breath.

The work carried out at Flint during that summer was not of a temporary nature. Massive ditches were dug and masons and carpenters brought in from the English Midlands. During the winter of 1277 to '78 a large part of the workforce was transferred to Rhuddlan, and we find them still hard at work there (Flint being by then sufficiently complete to be occupied) during the whole of 1278. Rhuddlan, though an ancient Norman seat, had recently been neglected in favour of the nearby castle at Dyserth, which Llywelyn had destroyed in 1263. From Edward's point of view Rhuddlan had the advantage that it could be supplied by sea, which Dyserth lacked. Indeed Dyserth (like Deganwy) was much too easy to besiege.

To consolidated this aspect of Rhuddlan's function Edward re-routed the river Clwyd, employing ditch-diggers brought from the fens of Lincolnshire to straighten its course through the marshes. This work, which took place during the period from November 1277 to the end of 1280, shows how serious Edward was in his scheme to make Rhuddlan the headquarters of his occupation of North Wales.

Edward was at Rhuddlan himself in August 1277, and remained there during that October and the first half of November. It was thus that Llywelyn came to him there, and it seems likely that the two men met then face to face for the first time.

Llywelyn came to Rhuddlan at the beginning of November, and the Treaty was signed at Aberconwy a few days later. It specified that although he was to retain the title of Prince, this was no longer to entitle him to allegiance from all other Welsh lords. These were allotted their realms, which they held by Edward's acquiescence, no longer by Llywelyn's. Most significantly his brother Dafydd was rewarded for having supported Edward in his invasion, being given lands in the Perfeddwlad, including the lordship of Hope, where he proceeded to build himself a castle, Caergwrle. Owain, Llywelyn's elder brother, was settled on the Lleyn peninsula. Llywelyn himself had his territory reduced to the inner heartland, the mountainous land across the Conwy, though he was also allowed to retain Anglesey, which the king had conquered, but now only as tenant-for-life.

The terms, severe though they were, could indeed have been worse. A substantial fine, as well as an annual rent for Anglesey, was discounted at once. Llywelyn probably could not have paid, but Edward could certainly have done with whatever he could get, after the enormously expensive campaign and with his still more costly building programme still in process. It is part of the evidence of Edward's strength that he was capable of great magnanimity.

One of the most surprising things about these last Plantagenet wars in Wales is that it is clear that Edward and Llywelyn liked each other. With equal implacability they had waited for the other to give way, and with equal unsuccess. Their arms-length confrontation and military engagement had no doubt fostered a mutual respect. Then finally they met, not as distantly opposed powers, but as people, when Llywelyn came to Rhuddlan offering submission. Strangely he seems to have gone from there having sown the seeds of a new friendship.

The king's first reaction was to invite his recent enemy to spend Christmas with him at Westminster. Perhaps it was more of an order than a suggestion, but for whatever reason Llywelyn (who had caused the war by refusing to go to London) went, and spent two weeks at court. He did the act of homage there which he had so adamantly refused. Perhaps he had no option, under the circumstances, but Edward certainly was not obliged to follow up their new association in the way he did.

Next time the king came to Rhuddlan, in September 1278, to supervise the works in progress there, the two leaders met again, in a meeting which was apparently most cordial. Quite soon afterwards, on 13th October, Edward went to extraordinary lengths to show Llywelyn his favour, by personally presenting him with his bride, the daughter of Simon de Montford whom he had previously withheld, at the door of Worcester cathedral. They then went through the formal marriage which had been postponed. Edward himself paid for the wedding-feast that night, and there was general rejoicing as the bride and groom went back Wales.

This complete apparent harmony, which testifies to the strength of character of both individuals, might have been the basis for a lasting peace. Indeed, in spite of the agenda implied by the continuing work at Rhuddlan and the harsh terms of the Treaty of Aberconwy, if it had been left to Edward and Llywelyn this might well have been the case. It was not Llywelyn who started the final war. It was his brother Dafydd.

The difference between the two brothers is significant to history, and Dafydd's persistent bitterness proved to be fatal to them both. He was apparently prepared to risk anything, including his country's future, in pursuit of an ideal of self-vindication. What is perhaps surprising is that Llywelyn allowed himself to get embroiled in his brother's quarrel, given the success with which he had assimilated his humiliating position, and the benefits which were now obvious in remaining on good terms with the English king.

Dafydd had been rewarded for his support of Edward by being made lord over two cantrefi of the Perfeddwlad, Rhufoniog and Dyffryn Clwyd. Yet he was not allowed the freedom to rule these that he reasonably expected. English officials, operating English, not Welsh, laws, interfered in his administration. He had in common with the population of the neighbouring cantrefi, which the king had kept for himself, that cause of resentment of royal intervention. The people of Wales as a whole smarted under alien rule, and Dafydd found himself in the odd position of being their representative.

It was on 21st March, 1282, which happened to be Palm Sunday: Dafydd led an attack on Hawarden Castle, one of the royal castles of the Marches. Llywelyn did not immediately respond to his brother's demand for assistance. Yet he was, after all, still officially Prince of Wales; and given the mood of his country he could not decently, or safely, side with the king against the people of Wales.

Dafydd attacked Hawarden from his base at Caergwrle, where now belated repairs have just about saved the crumbling remnant of his fortess on its crag. It was a surprise attack, and most of the garrison were killed before they could organise defence. They were, according to the English chronicler, slaughtered in their beds, 'both the young and old, women and children alike'. Though the English chronicle records that Llywelyn and Dafydd besieged Rhuddlan and Flint in the spring, and the Welsh one describes the breach launched by the Palm Sunday attack as being between Llywelyn and Edward, the historian John Davies considers that Llywelyn did not join Dafydd's revolt until June, by which time his wife had died in childbirth.

Edward was by all accounts astonished. Even so he acted with speed and determination, and by July the fleet was in the Dee estuary again, preparing for a return to Anglesey. The king was at Chester, where the army was mustering. The same month, July, he moved to Rhuddlan, which he then made his headquarters for the duration of the war. The fleet meanwhile had succeeded in taking Anglesey, and an attempt was made to attack Snowdonia from there, in the autumn of 1282.

This turned out to be something of a disaster. A bridge of boats was made across the Menai Strait (the English chronicler incorrectly says the River Conwy) which however collapsed, either through a misjudgement of the weight it would bear or of the strength of the tide. Alternatively the collapse is attributed to a doubling of the weight of knights crossing it, when those in front tried to turn back in panic at the approach of the Welsh from the other end. In either case encumbered by their armour they drowned, causing the loss of a significant part of the army.

Llywelyn himself was at his court at Aber at this time, and the Archbishop of Canterbury had come to him there on a peace mission, which, however, only had a slight delaying effect on the course of the war. The Archbishop shuttled backwards and forwards for a bit between Rhuddlan and Aber, but his efforts were in vain. The only terms which Edward would agree to Llywelyn could not accept. It would have involved giving up Wales and going into exile, and Llywelyn replied that the demands had amazed both him and his council. They would not have allowed him to consent to these even if he had wished to.

As the talks broke down, the bridge of boats had broken also in the Menai Strait, and Llywelyn was encouraged to emerge from the safety of Snowdonia, leaving Dafydd there to guard his retreat. It was November, and the two sides were set on a winter war.

This was not, however, what then took place. There is a slight, but tantalising, element of mystery about exactly what transpired. Llywelyn's death seems to have been to some extent an unplanned incident, rather than a part of the campaign. One of the versions of the 'Brut', the 'Red Book of Hergest' version, stops short of the event. The other, the Peniarth manuscript, gives more details of Llywelyn's movements.

When he emerged from the safety of Snowdonia he did not head towards Edward's army encamped at Rhuddlan. Instead he went into Powys, and concentrated on raising support in the lordship of Builth, presumably with the hope of outflanking the English alignment. A month elapsed, during which we only know of this movement in direction. It seems that the enemy, at least, did not know exactly where he was, since when he was killed they did not at first know that they had killed him.

The Peniarth manuscript describes the events as follows:

> And then Llywelyn ap Gruffydd left Dafydd, his brother, guarding Gwynedd, and he himself and his host went to gain possession of Powys and Builth . . . And then Roger Mortimer and Gruffydd ap Gwenwynwyn, and with them the king's host, came upon them without warning; and then Llywelyn and his foremost men were slain on the day of Damascus the Pope, a fortnight to a day from Christmas day; and that day was a Friday.

Roger Mortimer was in fact the son of his recently deceased first cousin, also Roger, since Llywelyn's father's sister had married into the Mortimer family. Another chronicle, which parallels the 'Brut', hints at a darker side to this encounter. The suggestion of treachery thus lies behind Llywelyn's death.

> And at that time the betrayal of Llywelyn was effected in the bellfries of Bangor by his own men. For at that time Llywelyn left Dafydd, his brother, to hold Gwynedd. And he himself and his host went to gain possession of Powys and Builth . . .

Implying that Roger Mortimer and Gruffudd ap Gwenwynwyn acted in some way with Dafydd's encouragement? The attack was plainly intended, yet it does not seem to have been directed against Llywelyn himself. He was not with the part of his forces which were initially attacked, and in the skirmish that followed a Shropshire foot soldier, Stephen Frankton, ran the prince through without knowing who he was. This was on 11th December, 1282, on the bank of the river Irfon, near Orewin bridge, in the area of Builth.

Once he was recognised Llywelyn's head was struck off and sent to London, where it was displayed on a lance at the Tower of London. His body was buried at the Cistercian abbey of Cwm Hir, at Maelienydd.

If this were a plot for his advancement, Dafydd did not gain by it. For a time he carried on the war. His weakness was that he could not command the allegiance which the Welsh had given to Llywelyn. Edward for his part did not then attempt to tackle the heartland of Snowdonia from the wrong bank of the Conwy. The most significant event in the last phase of the war was the fall of Dolwyddelan castle, on 18th January 1283, which enabled him to come down the Conwy valley on its western bank, his men cutting their way through the natural forest which still clothed its river bank. Thus he came to the haven of the Cistercians, the Abbey of Aberconwy, and he made that his headquarters while he tightened his grip on Snowdonia.

With an army in Anglesey pressing him in the foothills, and Edward controlling the Conwy river and the valley up to Dolwyddelan, Dafydd was effectively squeezed out of Snowdonia. He retreated to Castell y Bere, where he held out for a few months more. The Marcher and royal armies closed in on him, and his following was insufficient to provide him support in the country around. By April, 1283, there were 3,600 men surrounding Castell y Bere. Dafydd was in hiding in the hills, when his headquarters surrendered. The Welsh then joined in the hunt for their prince, and it was they who finally captured Dafydd, on the slopes of Cader Idris, on 28th June. He was sent to Shrewsbury, where he was tried for treason on 2nd October. Needless to say he was found guilty. Dafydd's long career of double-dealing had not in the end paid off. The English chronicle is harsh, but probably fair:

> He was a fomenter of evil, a most vicious tormentor of the English and deceiver of his own race, an ungrateful traitor and a war-mongerer.

Dafydd was dragged through the streets of Shrewsbury, hanged and then beheaded, finally quartered and disembowelled. His head was taken to London to stand on a stake next to his brother's in the Tower.

With the death of both the Princes the question of the inheritance of the title and the rights of Prince of Wales was effectively decided. Amongst the carefully considered terms of the Treaty of Aberconwy was a clause which made Edward Llywelyn's heir to the ownership of Anglesey, if Llywelyn died without issue. There were no male heirs to inherit what was left of Wales (Edward having already commandeered, by the same Treaty, much of the rest of it); but there was a daughter, Gwenllian, born in June 1282, just as Llywelyn was entering the final war. Her mother, Eleanor, died in childbirth, and Gwenllian was the only child Llywelyn had.

Edward took no chances with the possibility of succession. So that there should be no future heirs to the Princedom of Wales the tragic Gwenllian was taken to England and made to become a nun. The title itself Edward retained for the Crown, bestowing it on his son, Edward of Caernarfon, in 1301, when he was 17. It has ever since been the custom for the monarch to give the title to his or her eldest son.

In March, 1284, King Edward called a Parliament in Rhuddlan, where a plaque in the High Street marks the spot of his 'Parliament House'. On 19th March he issued a Statute from there, which marks the end of Wales' formal independence.

The Statue of Rhuddlan is largely a legal document, its most effective concern being to impose the laws of England on the newly-conquered territories; they already applied in much of the rest of Wales, which was governed by Marcher lords, and in the previously annexed royal lands. This was to finish the matter.

To a large extent the Statute of Rhuddlan is the documentary equivalent of the programme of castle-building which had already started, since its main impact was to set up a system of local administration; the castle towns were the embodiment of this, since they were necessary to house the administrators. Some of this system was not new: Edward used existing centres of the cantrefi, such as Cricieth and Bere, where he strengthened the castles, as well as new ones, such as Conwy. In Caernarfon and Harlech, where he started the process of building castles and walled boroughs in the summer of 1283, there had been administrative centres and therefore probably castles of a sort before, but Edward's work was entirely original on these sites. At Dolwyddelan he enlarged the castle as soon as he took it, in January 1283, but this did not proceed to the foundation of a borough. In Conwy, which was to be one of the major centres of the new administration, there was a preliminary problem. The great Abbey of Aberconwy had to be moved from the site of the proposed garrison town, because 'your Monastery for many reasonable causes could not remain conveniently in the place where it then was' (as the Papal Bull puts it), and Edward busied himself with the complexities of this upheaval during the end of 1283 and the early part of 1284. By the time the Statute of Rhuddlan was proclaimed the monastery had been moved wholesale to new premises at Maenan, in the middle Conwy valley, and work on the building of Conwy started at once.

The Statute of Rhuddlan set out the political future of North Wales, and it is in effect the instrument by which it is still governed. It appointed courts and officers, justices and sheriffs, responsible to the Crown. It laid out a framework based on the Norman shire system, by which the unit of administration, previously the cantrefi, became the counties, of Flint, Anglesey, Caernarfon, and Meirionnydd. This was not as radical a change as might have been expected, since the new shires still incorporated more local divisions, based on the old cantrefi, which in their turn reflected the ancient tribal divisions as they had become, over centuries, diffused into territorial clans. The power of clan-affiliation gradually weakened in most areas as the underpinning effect of the English legal system gained in strength.

On 25th April a son, the future Edward II, was born to Queen Eleanor at Caernarfon, where the royal couple had made their temporary home while the castle there was being built. In July Edward celebrated his conquest of Gwynedd in its innermost heart, at the old court of Nefyn, on the Lleyn peninsula, where he held a tournament and (with some sense of appropriateness) an Arthurian Round Table. Ironically it is the Welsh chronicler, rather than an English one, who provides this often strange story with its happy ending. Then:

> the king went happily jubilant to England, having conquered for himself all Gwynedd.

Bibliography

Chronicles, and John Davies, *A History of Wales*, as for previous chapters.
Chronicles of the Age of Chivalry. Ed. Elizabeth Hallam. Weidenfeld.
Oxford History of England: 'The Thirteenth Century'. Sir Maurice Powicke. Oxford, Clarendon.
An Historical Atlas of Wales. William Rees. Faber.
Castles of the Princes of Gwynedd. Richard Avent. HMSO.
The Welsh Castles of Edward I. Arnold Taylor. The Hambledon Press.
Dolwyddelan Castle, Dolbadarn Castle. Richard Avent. Cadw. *Cricieth Castle*. Richard Avent. Cadw.

Index